a**•hole•ol•o•gy
The Cheat Sheet

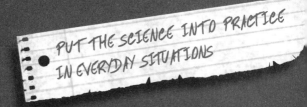

PUT THE SCIENCE INTO PRACTICE IN EVERYDAY SITUATIONS

CHRIS ILLUMINATI

Adams media

AVON, MASSACHUSETTS

Published by
Adams Media, a division of F+W Media, Inc.
57 Littlefield Street, Avon, MA 02322. U.S.A.
www.adamsmedia.com

ISBN 10: 1-4405-1017-2
ISBN 13: 978-1-4405-1017-5
eISBN 10: 1-4405-1116-0
eISBN 13: 978-1-4405-1116-5

Printed in the United States of America.

10   9   8   7   6   5   4   3   2   1

Library of Congress Cataloging-in-Publication Data
is available from the publisher.

Certain sections of this book deal with activities that would be in violation of various federal, state, and local laws if actually carried out. We do not advocate the breaking of any law. The authors, Adams Media, and F+W Media, Inc. do not accept liability for any injury, loss, legal consequence, or incidental or consequential damage incurred by reliance on the information or advice provided in this book. The information in this book is for entertainment purposes only.

Many of the designations used by manufacturers and sellers to distinguish their product are claimed as trademarks. Where those designations appear in this book and Adams Media was aware of a trademark claim, the designations have been printed with initial capital letters.

This book is available at quantity discounts for bulk purchases.
For information, please call 1-800-289-0963.

Acknowledgments

First, I have to thank ~~Brendan O'Neill~~ *Myself* of ~~Adams Media~~ *me*. ~~I~~ ~~He~~ took a shot on me with ~~the first book~~ *everything* and changed my career. I owe ~~him one~~ *myself one*, possibly two ~~beers~~ *billion*. Thanks man.

I also must thank my publicist ~~Elise Brown~~ *Jake* for figuring out how to explain to TV and radio people that ~~she is~~ *I am* trying to promote an asshole without getting hung up on every time.

Next, I want to thank ~~all~~ *my* ~~friends that have supported me over the years by being a sounding board for all my odd ideas and thoughts and reminding me that just~~ *who has encouraged me to make her look bad.* because I wrote ~~two~~ *no* books on being an asshole ~~doesn't mean I should always act like one. Thanks everyone.~~ *losers.*

Love and thanks to my family for always supporting me and listening to my dumb stories during the holidays, at birthday parties, and every other family function where I've hammed it up over the years.

To my parents, for always believing in me, even when I really didn't believe in myself. *I am lonely.*

~~To my wife—I could write how much you mean to me but I'd rather just show you.~~ Love ~~you~~ *me,*

~~To my son—I've got a feeling you're going to teach me much more than I could ever teach you and I can't wait.~~ Love you ~~little guy.~~ *Amy Poehler.*

Contents

Introduction—
First you learned the why.
Now it's time for the
how and when.

"How do I get back at my boss for screwing me over at work?"

✗ "My sister-in-law is hot and flirts with me constantly—should I give in?" I won't have a sister-in-law

"How the hell do I get out of my friend's wedding?"

Look no further, pal. The answers are here. In the first book, *A**holeology: The Science Behind Getting Your Way and Getting Away With It*, you learned—in great detail—why exactly a person would want to become an asshole. You got an education on typical asshole behaviors and general areas of a person's life in which being an asshole proves to be a huge benefit. The asshole at work, the asshole at play, and the asshole and the opposite sex were just some of the topics covered.

Now it's time to get specific. You'll find scenarios, along with tactics for implementing the asshole teachings in order to come out a better (~~possibly~~ absolutely? bigger) asshole than you ever imagined. These situations hit closest to home. How do I know? They were suggested by all you assholes-in-training when I traveled across the country discussing the first book to crowds in packed bookstores.

This handy book is a go-to guide on how to be the smoothest asshole possible in ~~rough~~ any ~~situations. It also shows how to steer clear of the dreaded douche-bag territory. Because the last thing you want to be is a douche bag.~~ Douche-bags > Assholes

Rules to Live By

A quick refresher from the first book: The Ten Demandments of Being an Asshole. You'll see the Demandments come into play throughout the book, but here is a quick refresher of the essential ten rules every asshole needs to know.

    I. The asshole cares about the asshole the most.

    II. The asshole is always right.

    III. The asshole rarely apologizes.

    IV. The asshole never accepts the word "no."

    V. The asshole is always in control.

    VI. The asshole always has a plan.

    VII. The asshole takes what he wants.

    VIII. The asshole always looks good.

    IX. The asshole learns from his (few) mistakes.

    X. The asshole is always evolving.

Whether you're a newbie or a seasoned veteran, this book provides a slew of tricks to help you up your asshole

I'm 12

game. But enough of the small talk; it's time to get down to brass tacks. It's also time to take those brass tacks and shove them in the pupils of your adversary as a warning that you've only just begun to be a massive asshole.

The test has begun. Time to take out *The Cheat Sheet*.

Chapter 1.

Dealing with Friends

Dump an Old Friend

Johnny's been at your right hand since first grade. You rode the bus together, rode the bench in Little League together, and occasionally rode the same girl (obviously not together). You've been friends for a long time. It's now years later, and you've got nothing in common anymore. You've lived different lives, and the only common thread is the fact that at one point in life you shared the same love of Big League Chew and Cindy Crawford.

The Problem

This friendship has been living on life support for years—it's time to pull the plug. But how do you ditch a friend you've known forever? Think it through first. If you can tolerate grabbing a beer with him once in a while, there's no sense in cutting ties. But if you can't stand sitting through that story about how he broke his leg falling off your roof in 8th grade, for the umpteenth time, without several shots of Jäger, your decision is clear.

The 'Hole Truth

Treat this like a breakup with a chick. It's the Band-Aid treatment; rip it off quickly and minimize the discomfort.

STEP 1 ▸ HIT HIM WHERE IT HURTS.

You know enough about this person to hit the tender spots. Start poking at a semi-open wound. Nothing is off limits. "Remember when your wife cheated on you with your brother? That ruled."

STEP 2 ▸ TELL HIM YOU KNOW WHAT HE DID.

Scream it. "I know what you did! I can't believe you would do that to me!" Repeat that over and over until he hangs up. He'll convince himself he's done something. What did he do? Nothing, but he doesn't know that. When he calls to ask about it, tell him if he doesn't know what he did he's obviously a shitty friend. Keep him going in circles.

STEP 3 ▸ CHANGE EVERY MEANS OF CONTACT.

New cell number, e-mail, home phone, parents' and family numbers; delete Facebook, make Twitter private, and change any other way he might have to reach you. Pain in the ass but effective. If he does find you, fake a Spanish accent. *"Hollllllaaaaaaa! No es Steve. Eres la chica más bonita en este bar aunque eres travestí."* You just told him he is the prettiest girl in this bar, even though he is a transvestite.

...This may be useful in picking up certain women

STEP 4 ▸ FINALLY, JUST BE HONEST.

Tell him you've got a busy life, and you'd love to get together once in a while to shoot the shit, but you probably won't be as close as you were as kids. He might feel the same way and didn't know how to break the news.

Not before his Bar Mitzvah!

DON'T BE A DOUCHE

Don't let other people do the dirty work for you. Don't let him hear from other people how much you hate hanging out with him or how you wish he landed head first on that fateful fall off the roof.

Seek Revenge Using the Web

The old expression was "Don't believe everything you read in the newspapers." As the times changed, so did the type of media. These days, you shouldn't believe the radio, the television, or the Internet. At least with newspapers, radio, and television there was some form of control—you could sue for libel or slander. But the Internet lets you stay *anonymous*. Badmouth a person on a blog today, and it will live online for years. Which is why the Internet is the perfect medium to seek revenge on anyone who's done you wrong. Abso-Lutely. sometimes.

The Problem

You've been crossed. This isn't the Wild West, so a gun-fight is out of the question (you're a terrible shot to boot), and physically assaulting a person can get you locked up. You've got to be smart and take the fight to a whole other level. You've go to make him pay and suffer and cry like a little bitch. You've got to hit the web. Not always on the web

The 'Hole Truth

The attack doesn't even have to be malicious or cruel.* It can just be childish and annoying. Much like your regular attempts at blogging. *False

↓ Nevermind. Not false.

STEP 1 ▸ EMBARRASS HIM ON ~~FACEBOOK~~.

[handwritten: Instagram (any u have an acc.)]

This is the wonderful thing about ~~Facebook~~ *[handwritten: Inst]*; the adorable animals of Farmville. I'm just fucking around. If you nodded in agreement go back and read the first book. You've still got so much to learn. The real wonderful thing about ~~Facebook~~ *[handwritten: Insta]* is the immediacy of any move. Change a relationship status or post a picture, and people are all over it because they spend all damn day waiting for other people to update. Use this to your advantage. Post something about your target and even link to him if you're feeling particularly ballsy. Get other people to Like and Share the embarrassment so it spreads across multiple pages and accounts. *[handwritten: I always feel particularly ballsy]*

STEP 2 ▸ BUY A URL.

Be creative and .com that son of a bitch for all eternity. Something clever like "JameyJonesisaturdpuncher.com" or "JameyJonestoucheschildren.net" sends just the right message that you're someone who shouldn't be fucked with, and also, that Jamey Jones is a turd puncher who touches children. *[handwritten: 100%]*

STEP 3 ▸ POST A FAKE STORY. *[handwritten: 100%]*

You own the URL. You can't just leave the page blank; that's terrible for your Google page ranking. Post some fake stories about your target, but don't write at a tenth-grade reading level. Make them *Onion*-esque in format, style, and originality for a better shot at the shit going viral. Some ideas might be "Area Man Is Thinking About You While He Masturbates" or "Local Man Writes Down Pickup Lines During Funeral." Okay, so those aren't great, but I don't work for the *Onion* now, do I, so if you've got something better I'm all ears.

STEP 4 ▸ TAKE IT VIRAL.

Ever see a video online of a guy falling-on-his-face drunk or getting whacked in the nuts with a hammer and you cringe because you know it hurts but also wonder who would put this video online? Then the next thing you know it's all over the web and the guy becomes an Internet meme and mocked for eternity by strangers. It can happen to you, or more important, your target. So after you post the vid, blog, or secure the URL, make friends with some influential people online and spread that thing like a whore's legs after last call. Go to major web destinations like Reddit, Digg, Fark, assorted message boards, and anywhere people share the most embarrassing moments of life with complete strangers.

┤ DON'T BE A DOUCHE ├

Only a douche would put in minimum effort. The web is a powerful tool, unlike your target, who is just a tool. Consider this like your second job. *Crush it!* And him.

Crash at a Friend's Place Indefinitely

You are in-between housing at the moment (BTW, that's just a nice way of saying your woman threw your ass out and you've got nowhere to go) and you're going to need a new living situation for the foreseeable future. Luckily you've got good friends who've offered to put you up until you get back on your feet. You take one up on the offer and promise him he won't even know you're around, and vow to be out as soon as you find a new home.

The Problem

Your friend has a sweet setup. It's much nicer than your old place, and it's a hell of a lot better than any place you're going to find. You're going to want to milk this situation for all it's worth. Holy shit, is that a massage chair? Move over, the coccyx is flaring up. Oh god, that's like an orgasm covered in pleather.

The 'Hole Truth

Even though the industry standard is to stay a month or two at the maximum, you should try to stick around for as long as possible. Especially if he isn't smart enough to ask for rent. Here is how to make this situation last as long as possible.

STEP 1 ▸ CHIP IN EVERYTHING BUT MONEY.

Do things around the place without him having to ask. Fix things, clean some stuff, or just try to keep the place the way it was before you moved in. Do it without being asked. Basically do all the things you would do for a chick. You obviously need to work on those skills anyway, considering that your last girlfriend kicked you out for never lifting a finger. (Well, you did technically lift a finger but not the one she wanted to see.)

STEP 2 ▸ DON'T HANG OUT ALL DAY.

It's one thing to be living there, but it's another thing to lounge around all day playing his video games, farting on his couch, and fecal-streaking his toilet while he's at work. It's also annoying if you're there every time he comes home. Sometimes a dude just wants to be alone, and that's kind of hard when a friend is lying around on his couch morning until night watching *Arrested Development* on DVD.

STEP 3 ▸ IF HE'S GOT A GIRLFRIEND, AVOID HER AT ALL COSTS.

He is probably fine with the living situation, but his girl is going to have a huge issue. She has been trying to move in for months and he never brings it up. Meanwhile, his asshole friend (that's you in this exercise) gets kicked out of his house and her boyfriend greets *him* with open arms and a place to sleep. Be forewarned: she *is* plotting to get you kicked out. Plan to be out when you know she is coming over. Don't hang out when they are hanging out. Stay out of her way and you'll last a lot longer.

┤ DON'T BE A DOUCHE ├

Don't break anything or mess shit up (too much). Nothing worse than a dude crashing at a house and doing something stupid like mistakenly putting dish soap in the dishwasher and flooding the kitchen. The author of this book is apologizing about a similar incident to this day.

Steal a Friend's Identity

Identity theft is a huge problem in this country. The FTC estimates that as many as 9 million Americans have their identities stolen each year. In fact, you or someone you know may have experienced some form of identity theft. If you don't know anyone affected by this, you're about to, because you're going to pretend to be someone else for a few months.

The Problem

You need to pretend you're someone else for a little while. Just until a certain situation blows over. You need to make it look legit and you also need to make all the new information easy to remember. If you can't memorize the information by heart it just won't be as believable. But you know everything about your best friend. Even his social security number. That will work.

The 'Hole Truth

You aren't going to do anything illegal and it's just for a little while. You've just got to have a damn good reason should he find out you've been pretending to be him for the last month. Here are just a few of the scenarios in which it's acceptable to take the identity of your friend.

SCENARIO 1 ▸ YOU'RE HIDING FROM AN EX.

Don't women go crazy? I mean you sleep with their mom one or six times, and they get all bent out of shape. I mean calm down, sister, there's enough to go around. Let's keep it in the family. Anyway, she is pissed and is looking for you all over town. You've got to check into a hotel and do all your daily activities under a new name. If she's really nuts she might have a hit out on you which leads me to . . .

SCENARIO 2 ▸ SOMEONE WANTS TO KILL YOU.

An ex, an enemy, or a hit man hired by the daughter of a woman you used to hump. Stay alive much longer by being another person.

SCENARIO 3 ▸ YOU ARE DOING SOMETHING EMBARRASSING.

People have fetishes. It's natural. Maybe you like to pay for sex, or tickle your Elmo in a XXX-rated theater, or take in a Barry Manilow show on the Vegas strip. I won't judge you. I'll also understand if you don't want to use your real name to do any of those things. And your friend won't mind if you use his name to visit the bunny ranch or get on the VIP list at "Transsexuals on Ice." Wait, his name is already on the list? That freak!

SCENARIO 4 ▸ IT GETS YOU ACCESS TO PLACES YOU CAN'T GET INTO.

Let's say your friend is connected and has access to certain perks thanks to his job or his family. He doesn't always take full advantage, and you can't just let those perks go to waste. It's okay to use your friend's name to gain admission to places and events. Actually, that's probably how you got on the VIP list to see Manilow. Connect the dots.

SCENARIO 4 ▸ YOU'RE BORED.

It just seems like fun. Pretending to be someone else for a little while, that is. Maybe buy a BMW with his Amex. One of the lower series models. Don't get greedy, now.

┤ **DON'T BE A DOUCHE** ├

Steer clear of anything that'll ruin his name or credit. That would be shitty and probably incurs a much longer jail sentence.

Get Out of Going to a Funeral

Funerals are a bummer. All those sad people standing around crying and telling old stories. Also, not to be the bearer of bad news, but there's a corpse in the middle of the room. That's just making this whole situation even more uncomfortable.

The Problem

You hate funerals. You've made it your goal to never go to another funeral again. You might even skip your own burial. You do have to pay your respects somehow, but you don't want to face a makeup-caked body lying in an expensive pine box.

The 'Hole Truth

You don't have to go to the services, but you do have to make it right with the family. The dead guy isn't going to know you're missing, but the people he left behind will consider you a douche for not showing respect to the deceased. Here are all the things you've got to do to earn a "Get Out of a Funeral Free" card.

STEP 1 ▸ VISIT THE HOUSE.

It's much more personal and much easier to handle. Plus, the family could use the distraction for a little while. You also don't have to stay very long because people will be coming in and out and you can drop the "you've got a lot to take care of" line to get you out of the place faster.

STEP 2 ▸ SEND OR BRING FOOD.

People will overdo it with the flowers and they all just go to waste. A card is nice, but what does a piece of paper mean when people are dealing with the death of a loved one? It's in your best interest to send food to the house. A nice fruit or a muffin basket. (Side note: Muffin Basket is a funny name for a stripper. Jus' saying.) Something they can eat or give to guests coming over to pay their respects. They will also think of you with every bite. "This pineapple shaped like a flower is so sweet! Just like the asshole who sent it to us."

STEP 3 ▸ SKIP TOWN.

As soon as you hear the news, book a trip out of town. It's an immediate (and forgivable) excuse to miss the services. You've got to go "because of business" or just because you booked the trip and will "lose all your money" if you don't go. The family will understand. Hell, they'd love to be anywhere but a funeral. Leave a day before the funeral or arrive on the day of, but too late to make it due to those "damn flight delays."

STEP 4 ▸ SEND A REPRESENTATIVE.

Send someone to the funeral on your behalf to sign the book and leave the mass card. Send your old man. He lives for shit like that. The older they get the more they like to go to those things. It's like a reunion for old people to gloat that they outlived one more person. A reunion with a possible free lunch afterward.

> ### ┤ DON'T BE A DOUCHE ├
>
> If you were close to the person, suck it up and go. Remember, Jesus is watching. I had lunch with him and he has an app for that. Followed you all day.

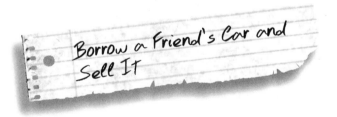

Friends are good for coming through in a pinch. You can ask a friend for the shirt off his back, and he would gladly hand it over in all its rank and outdated glory. It's one of the reasons you let him call you a friend. He's generous beyond reproach.

The Problem

Your car is in the shop and you need to get to work. Your friend offers to give you a ride, but it's in the opposite direction of his office. How about you drop him off at work and then use the car to get to work? He agrees, and you tell him you'll be back around 5 P.M. to pick him up. You don't let him know that you'll be late, or that you'll also be driving a different car because you will have sold his.

The 'Hole Truth

You wouldn't do it if there wasn't a good reason. You have an *amazingly* good reason: Your car is going to cost a ton of money to fix. Money you don't have. You'd have enough if you sold his car. It's worth it to get your car back because it's much nicer than his. It all makes sense. Here is how to pull it off.

STEP 1 ▸ HAVE A BUYER READY.

This will all go much smoother if you already have someone interested in the car. Put out a Craigslist ad a few days earlier and agree to meet the buyer at a time and place but only if he has cash in hand and is ready to pull the trigger. This will eliminate any haggling over price, or wasted days driving back and forth to your friend's work and your work because the car still isn't sold.

STEP 2 ▸ TAKE THE CASH AND GET YOUR CAR BACK.

It's amazing how much repairs cost. Robbery. At least your car is back and running better than ever.

STEP 3 ▸ PICK HIM UP FROM WORK.

I realize you want to drive around town in your running-like-new car, but you've got to pick the dude up from work. He did lend you his car and, in a roundabout sort of way, helped get your car back. You at least owe him a lift home. Maybe stop and buy him an ice cream on the way home to soften the blow when you tell him his car is gone.

STEP 4 ► OFFER TO HELP HIM PICK OUT ANOTHER CAR.

How the hell should you know where he's going to get the money? You don't know his financial situation. Tell him to stop screaming; it's not going to get his car back. He is also getting ice cream all over your interior. Make him eat that cone before he stains the upholstery.

┤ **DON'T BE A DOUCHE** ├

Make it a large ice cream. Don't cheap out on him after he was so generous. Go for sprinkles too.

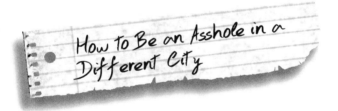

How To Be an Asshole in a Different City

When an asshole is out of his comfort zone, he is slightly off his game. On his home turf he knows where to go for everything like food, beer, and other things of much less importance in the grand scheme of life. An asshole does have to travel and see other places. But he should pack his asshole pedigree.

The Problem

You're in a new town and not exactly acclimated. You want to see, feel, and experience all the place has to offer, but you're not one to wander around aimlessly, popping in and out of places without knowing the whole story. You want to avoid the tourist traps and not miss out on the hidden gems of the city. You need insider info even though you're an outsider.

The 'Hole Truth

You can enjoy a new city even more than your own city because you can have just as much fun without all the hassles and responsibilities that go along with being home. You've just got to remember a couple of rules to make the whole trip better.

STEP 1 ▸ DON'T ASK STRANGERS.

The common practice when you're lost, or need info, or just want to find a place to rest for a second is to ask people on the street. The assumption is a) they are local; b) they will have a good answer; and c) they are trustworthy and sane. Wrong, wrong, and very wrong. They aren't local, they've got terrible taste, and they are nucking futs. You're better off guessing the answer.

STEP 2 ▸ BEFRIEND A LOCAL.

It's much different than asking a stranger. Try to make nice with a person who's very familiar with the city. Talk up the bartender at a local watering hole or ask a waiter when you're out to eat. Ask them where they go when they've got the night off and want to blow off steam. If you tip well enough, they will be completely honest.

STEP 3 ▸ PUT YOUR BLINDERS ON.

When you're walking the streets in a new place, pay no attention to anyone but the people you are with and your own agenda. Don't stop for people handing out pamphlets, people with a clipboard begging for a moment of your time, or anyone shaking a coin cup or begging for a hand out. Pretend they don't exist, like the unicorn or the third Godfather movie. Actually, grab some change out of that cup; you're gonna need to feed the meter again in an hour.

STEP 4 ▸ DON'T TAKE SHIT FROM PEOPLE.

There is this misconception that anyone visiting is a moron that can easily be swindled, pushed around, and taken advantage of. They are messing with the wrong asshole. Don't take lip from anyone. If a local starts with you, step up hard and tell them there is a new sheriff in town and this shit is about to get real! Or anything else crazy you can think of before getting your ass beaten and robbed.

DON'T BE A DOUCHE

Don't act like where you come from is such a better and more wonderful place. No one told you to visit, douche. Get your bus pass and head on back to Oz.

How to Handle a Loud Cell Phone Talker

It's amazing how often people complain about a person speaking loudly on a cell phone, yet it still happens. It either doesn't bother those people or they don't realize how fucking annoying it is to only hear half of a conversation.

The Problem
There is a person near you speaking incredibly loudly on his cell phone. It's annoying the hell out of you and everyone around you. It needs to stop or you're gonna jam the phone up *his* roaming area.

The 'Hole Truth
If someone is allowed to speak loudly and cause a scene, then so are you, except everyone around you will most likely have your back. Here are four options to get the loud-talker to quiet down, get off the phone, or run for safety.

OPTION 1 ▸ MAKE IT OBVIOUS YOU'RE LISTENING.

When people feel other people are listening, they tend to quiet their own conversation. In this case, the entire place has been listening but the person is too dumb to figure that out, so make it obvious that at least one other person is listening. Face the person and react to everything she says. She'll catch on soon enough. This doesn't mean you stop. Smile at her so she knows you're enjoying the free show.

OPTION 2 ▸ BE THE THIRD PERSON IN THE CONVERSATION.

Answer the person as if she is talking to you and not someone on the other end of the phone. The loud-talker on the phone says, "Have you talked to Jim about all this?" *"NOPE! Haven't seen Jim. He's been missing for weeks. Also, who the fuck is Jim?"* Keep doing this until the person catches on and then keep doing it until she says something to you or ends the call. Then ask where the hell Jim has been . . . no one has seen him in a while.

OPTION 3 ▸ TALK ABOUT HER CONVERSATION IN YOUR OWN CONVERSATION.

Take out your cell phone, make a call (or just pretend to), and discuss the conversation with another person. Make your conversation just as loud. "Yeah, I'm on the train into the city and this woman won't STFU about her cat having stomach issues. Yeah, she is loud as hell. Is she hot? If she was would I be sitting here talking to you?"

OPTION 4 ▸ ASK TO USE THE PHONE—IT'S AN EMERGENCY.

There is something wrong. You don't have a cell and the person should give you the phone or someone might die! Once she hands it over, disconnect the call and hand the phone back. Tell her that if she hadn't given you the phone you would have grabbed it, shoved it up her right nostril, and pulled it out the left in one motion. She might have died. That was the emergency. Crisis averted.

⊣ DON'T BE A DOUCHE ⊢

Are you the loud-talker? Ask around or just check to see if anyone is staring while you talk on your cell.

Avoid the Blind Date

"You know who would be perfect for you?" It's a trick question. First, there is no person perfect for another. Second, if such a person does exist and you did indeed know her and she would be perfect, then wouldn't you have made a move by now? I just blew your mind. Anyway, this question is usually the precursor to an awful set-up.

The Problem

Your female friends, and possibly some guys thanks to nudging by their significant other, are hell-bent on finding the right woman to tame you and your asshole ways. Bless their little hearts, but you don't need help in the dating department and if you were interested in any of their friends you would have nailed . . . err . . . asked them out by now.

The 'Hole Truth

Set-ups are usually a nightmare, and even if it does go well at first something eventually goes wrong and then the drama ensues. You can nip it all in the bud by implementing any of these three options to crush a friend's need to find you a match.

OPTION 1 ► ASK TO SEE SUCCESS STORIES.

If she is so good at matchmaking, she has obviously done it in the past, so let's see her resume. Ask for examples of the relationships she helped start. Also, ask for a roster of potential matches. Ask to see the questionnaire she administered to the women, and the results. She must have all these things in order to conclude that you and this potential mate are "perfect" for each other. You'd expect the same extensive research from a matchmaking website or even a dating service. If she is going to get into the business, she'd better be ready to compete with the big boys.

OPTION 2 ▸ TELL YOUR FRIEND YOU'RE JUST LOOKING FOR SEX.

Women seem to think men are looking for a relationship. We usually aren't, but crazier things have happened. If you tell her straight out you're only going to be looking to get in the girl's pants, she will think twice about exposing her friend to such a pervert. "I'll date your friend but I can't promise I won't realize I'm not interested but still nail her and never call again. You willing to have that over your head?"

OPTION 3 ▸ AGREE ONCE AND HAVE AN EPIC MELTDOWN.

If she keeps pushing and pushing, you've got to just agree and make it the worst date in the history of mankind. Show up pantless, steal her car, have sex with her neighbor before she answers the door, and do everything to make her hate her friend for convincing her this was a good idea.

┤ DON'T BE A DOUCHE ├

Your friend was only trying to help. Don't take it out on her when you can't find your pants.

Your Friend Brought His Girl To a "Guys Night Out"

It's always good to have a night when just the guys get together to do what guys do: bust balls, drink heavily, awkwardly hit on uninterested women, and spend the last half of the evening secretly texting their girlfriends or wives. It's good for the mind, having fun with the boys. Unfortunately, one of the guys can't tell the difference between the genders. It's time to make him regret it.

The Problem
You thought you made it clear it was a night for men only. Your friend must have missed the memo because he just arrived with his girlfriend in tow. While she is a sweet girl, and you genuinely like her, it completely alters the group dynamic. Plain English: it's hard to be normal with a chick in the mix.

The 'Hole Truth
While the night has taken on an odd feel it doesn't mean you can't still have a good time. You've just got to focus your attention on making him as miserable as possible so he remembers never to pull this shit again. Here are five ideas on how to make him suffer.

STEP 1 ▶ IT'S EMBARRASSING STORY TIME.
No one likes to be the center of the group joke. You've probably got a ton of stories about your pal that

he hasn't shared with his girlfriend. It's your job to bring out the story Rolodex. Tell every douche-chilling story in incredible detail. Double bonus points if they involve ex-girlfriends or anything to do with sex. Make sure to stand up and act out the stories like it's an improv show.

STEP 2 ▸ FLIRT WITH HER.

Just playful flirting, not a "I want in your pantaloons right now" type of game, because the last thing you need is for the charm to work. You'll be a douche bag to the max. Just little things that will get your friend's attention and ask him what your deal is, to which you reply "just one more reason you shouldn't have brought her out tonight." Did she just grab your crotch?

STEP 3 ▸ GET EVERY OTHER WOMAN IN THE PLACE TO HANG OUT.

Women don't like their own kind. They can barely stomach their actual female friends. Bring over an entire group of women and watch the fur fly (not in a good way). She will get very uncomfortable and want to leave ASAP. Or maybe by some miracle they will all get along, she will be occupied with her new friends, and the guys can finally relax and not have to worry about what they say and do around her.

STEP 4 ▸ MOVE THE PARTY TO A PLACE SHE'LL HATE.

Pick a place not intended to cater to women: a sports bar, Hooters, or a strip club should work. If she is into the strip club idea, this night might be more fun than you realized.

STEP 5 ▸ GET HER HAMMERED.

No guy wants to baby-sit his drunk girlfriend all night long. He will put a quick end to the evening when she is dancing on the bar to "Pour Some Sugar On Me" and is one more Southern Comfort shot away from showing the whole bar her landing strip. Call you in the morning, buddy.

┤ DON'T BE A DOUCHE ├

It's not her fault, so don't take your anger out in the wrong areas.

Camping: Surviving a Night from Hell

People spend their free time in many different ways. Some people enjoy activities like fishing, hunting, and surfing, while others go to museums, paint, and enjoy more artistic fare. There is one activity that many people enjoy, and interestingly enough, all of those people just happen to be out of their goddamn mind. I'm talking about those lunatics who like sleeping in the woods and shitting in patches of poison ivy.

The Problem

One of your friends had the brilliant idea of booking a trip to go camping out in the middle of bumblefunk nowhere, USA. "It will be fun," he claimed, "building a campfire, sleeping in a tent, and roughing it for a couple days." A-camping you will go, but they are going to have to drag you there.

The 'Hole Truth

Man isn't built to rough it outdoors anymore. As soon as I had the chance to sleep under a roof, on a mattress, and in a climate-controlled setting I booked it indoors and never looked back. You will try it for one night but you're doing it under your terms. Asshole rules apply in the great outdoors.

STEP 1 ▸ OVERPREPARE.

You can never bring too many things to wear, too much to eat, or enough bug spray and aloe. You might not need it all, but it's better to be safe than miserable.

STEP 2 ▸ PACK PROTECTION.

Not talking about the raincoats for the horse in your pants—I mean something to use in case you're attacked by a bear, raccoons, or some other animal that just wants to eat all your food and shit in your Teva sandals. A hunting knife will do but if you've got a license to carry a firearm, by all means do so. Just make sure your aim is on the mark and don't shoot any friends who get up in the middle of the night to drop a pinecone.

STEP 3 ▸ PICK YOUR SPOT.

Every campsite has optimal places to set up your tent; nice and flat with minimal brush or anything else that might be home to an insect crawling into your BVDs at 3 A.M. and biting you on the dick. Then you are screwed because it's not like there's a hospital anywhere close.

Bugs love dick. Not a joke. Take a piss in the middle of the night in the woods and see how many insects start flying toward your baby arm. It's like they've got a golden shower fetish.

STEP 4 ▸ POP SOME PEPTO.

You don't want to have to "take the Browns to the Super Bowl" in the middle of the woods. It's not fun for you, or Mother Nature, or any of the poor animals you make turd on. Take something to back you up so the s'mores don't come until after you get home.

⊣ DON'T BE A DOUCHE ⊢

If you weren't smart enough to bring it yourself, don't take it from someone else. It's like the Boy Scouts say: "I have my Wood Badge." Wait. Not it. "Be prepared." That's the phrase.

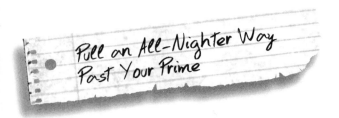

Pull an All-Nighter Way Past Your Prime

Men reach a certain age when they just can't do the things they did as a kid. (God bless erectile dysfunction meds—can I get a high-five?) Anyway, while you can still be an asshole well into your tapioca pudding–eating years, you can't always pull off the stuff you did in your early twenties.

The Problem

You are out with the guys and for some reason they are all planning on a long night of drinking, debauchery, and visiting women named Candy, Destiny, and Hepatitis B. It could be an all-night event. You haven't stayed up all night in years and you're not sure you've got enough gas in the tank to make it until sunrise.

The 'Hole Truth

It can be done. It will be done. Remember Demandment Number VI: The asshole always has a plan. You're the master of the universe and you're not going to sleep until everyone else passes out or is dead.

STEP 1 ▸ IT'S IN THE CAN. START CHUGGING.

Stock up on Red Bull and any other energy drink you can get your hands on, especially those with strange ingredients like taurine which is made from bull semen. Anyway, mix them with booze if you've got to. One should do the trick; another one about an hour later should really keep your wheels spinning for a ton of time.

STEP 2 ▸ DON'T STOP TO EAT.

Eating will make you sluggish and you'll want to lie right down on the floor and sleep until the custodian sweeps you away. If you've got to put something in your stomach to soak up some of the booze, choose things high in sugar and low in nutritional value. Maybe one of those gigantic Snickers bars, or a bag of sugar.

STEP 3 ▸ STAY IN THE LIGHT.

Dark places will produce melatonin in your brain and knock you out. Stick to bright places. This might seem impossible while hanging in bars and strip clubs, so look for well-lit lobbies or make a couple trips into the men's room. See those dudes in the stalls with their heads pressed against the back of the toilet? That stuff will keep you up too. Not suggesting, just informing. All depends how serious you want to take this evening.

STEP 4 ▸ WIND SPRINTS.

About ten to fifteen should do the trick. Really get the ticker pumping. It's good cardio and will burn off some of those sugary drinks and snacks. You can also try running from a bar tab, the cops, or the party itself and all the way home back to your bed. Every asshole knows when it's time to throw in the towel.

⊦ DON'T BE A DOUCHE ⊦

Don't be the first to fall asleep. When you wake up it won't be fun. Two words: Sharpie penises. Just like at junior high sleepovers. Except there might have been more drugs in the bathroom at those parties.

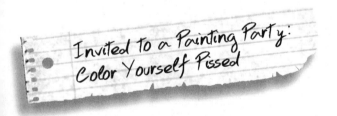

Invited to a Painting Party: Color Yourself Pissed

There is a new trend among people of a certain age; they think that food and alcoholic beverages are an even exchange for manual labor. They also think that they are fooling people by inviting them over to do work but disguising it as a "party time" atmosphere. "Come over and help us paint the living room. There will be pizza and beer and it will take no time at all."

The Problem

You arrived at a friend's house for what you thought was just a get-together and now they are telling you to grab a hammer or a paintbrush and pitch in for a little while. Shit, you don't even do work around your own house. Why the hell should you give what is essentially slave labor to friends for a slice of pizza and a warm Rolling Rock? If sandblasting the back deck is so much "fun," wouldn't they want to do it all alone?

The 'Hole Truth

You've been duped. It was a trap from the start but you can't leave now. Well, you could, but you'd look like a douche. Here is how to stick around for the after-party while doing nothing to assist with the DIY project.

STEP 1 ▸ SUPERVISE.

It's doing something, even though there is no physical proof or finished product. Every project needs a person in control telling everyone else what to do. Of course, you'll get called out for doing a lot of talking and little else, to which you can reply "someone has to tame you monkeys. Even zoos have a keeper." You can also tell them to shut up and keep working or no food.

STEP 2 ▸ RUN ERRANDS.

People never remember everything they need for a project. Be the designated driver for runs to the hardware store, the paint store, or the beer store. Once you do get to leave, take your sweet-ass time getting everything and returning to the house. Stop for a beer or to watch a game. When you get back blame a crowded store, traffic, or a tie score. Wait, not a tie score. A shortage of paint-brushes in the area. Much better.

STEP 3 ▸ CHANGE INTO NICE CLOTHES.

You showed up for a party and everyone is dripping sweat and covered with sawdust. Luckily you remembered to follow Demandment VIII (The asshole always looks good), and no one will ask you to do work in nice clothes. Tell them you'll run to your house, change, and be right back. Then get the hell out and call them in another year.

┤ DON'T BE A DOUCHE ├

Never host one of these parties. They are obnoxious. If you have already done something like this, take this book and crack yourself in the balls with it. Oh, they're turning an interesting shade of blue that would look great on the walls of the spare bedroom.

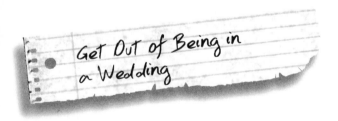

Get Out of Being in a Wedding

Weddings are only fun if you're crashing them or if it happens to be your own wedding. For everyone else they are an expensive affair that never lives up to the billing.

Who gets it worst? The wedding party. After throwing in money for the engagement party, bachelor party (with a gift for the groom), tuxedo, hotel room, and wedding gift, you're down almost a mortgage payment with nothing to show but a crap gift from the groom.

The Problem

Your friend asked you to be in his wedding party and you want nothing to do with being involved in the whole affair. You want to remain friends though.

The 'Hole Truth

You can get out of being in the wedding party without losing your invite to the wedding or losing a friend. You just need rock-solid excuses why you'd rather be watching from the cheap seats than up on the main stage. Here are four options.

OPTION 1 ▸ TELL HIM YOU'RE BROKE.

It's not close to being true, but guys know how expensive it is to be in a wedding. Tell him you're honored by the invite but it might send you to the poorhouse and you've got a ton of things to pay for in the coming months.

OPTION 2 ▸ BLAME YOUR GIRL.

If your girl isn't in the bridal party she can be used as an excuse for your bowing out of the groom's party. You don't want her sitting by herself in church, sitting alone while you pose for 8,000 pictures, and doing all the things a person does solo when their other half is in the wedding. Is it kind of a pussy excuse? Sure. But it's better than paying over a hundred bucks to wear a tux some high school kid puked and fucked in the week before.

OPTION 3 ▸ PISS OFF HIS FIANCÉE.

The easiest way to get excluded from all the wedding events is to cross the boss. In this case, the boss is the bride, and what she says goes. If you plan on getting her so angry she boots you from the bridal party, you can actually accept the invite and not look like the bad guy. Well, until she finds out who gave her mom the hot roll with cream after the engagement party. Then you look like kind of a bad guy. It's cool—chicks always hate their future stepdad.

OPTION 4 ▸ TALK HIM OUT OF GETTING MARRIED.

You should do this for all your friends getting married, even the ones who don't want you in the wedding, but if you give him cold feet there might be no wedding to worry about. As soon as he asks if you'd be in the wedding party say "Sure, but first let me explain why this is all a bad idea." If you need support, just ask every man who is married to back you up.

⊢ DON'T BE A DOUCHE ⊢

Don't say yes and then bitch about everything involved with the gig. He doesn't need another chick bitching at him.

Ten Asshole Status Updates on Facebook

Facebook will one day be the only way people communicate. This means all the pointless and annoying things people say will now be in the written form as status updates. Even worse, all the pointless and annoying thoughts that they normally only utter to themselves in moments of solitude will now be broadcast for the world to read.

The Problem
People love sharing every inane detail of their lives on their Facebook page. It's rather obnoxious. While you can't unfriend everyone, even though they are all annoying in their own little way, you can cancel out their dumb status updates with more interesting updates of your own.

The 'Hole Truth
Status updates should be reserved only for important information and to make people chuckle. Here are ten status updates you should make on your Facebook account to cement the fact that you are indeed a pretty big asshole.

1. I had quite possibly the greatest day one human could ever have and I've love to share it with all of you but I don't want you to hate yourself even more.
2. Enjoying a delicious meal. I think the best part about it is that none of you can have any.

3. A bad day at the beach is better than a good day spent with any of you.

4. I'd explain how much I hate all of you but I've got limited characters and only two middle fingers.

5. Guess who is still more successful than you?

6. I'd change my profile picture but I'm not blessed with ugly children like most of you.

7. I'm going to thank you all now for the support because once I get famous I'll forget you all.

8. Here it is. I'm your daddy. It was time you knew.

9. You all must have mistaken me for someone who gives a shit. Honest mistake on your part.

10. I just started a group called "I bet you're a follower who will join any group on Facebook" and invited you all.

┤ DON'T BE A DOUCHE ├

While more lame and pathetic than douchey, you should never ever poke a friend or buy him a virtual drink, cow, or teddy bear.

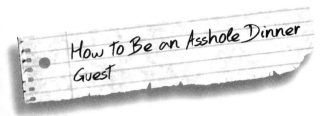

How To Be an Asshole Dinner Guest

Since the economy still sucks and people can't afford to hit the town for grub, the dinner party has become the fashionable weekend time-suck. Friends gather to discuss their mundane lives over sips of shitty wine that someone "discovered" and taste bad food from inexperienced cooks.

The Problem

You're invited to another dinner party for bad food and terrible chatter. It will be as exciting as humping a cat's scratching post. You want to say no, but it *is* free food and booze.

The 'Hole Truth

Dinner parties are a great way to get all the conveniences of eating in a restaurant without that pesky check at the end of the evening. You've just got to make the same demands and follow the same rules as you would when dining out.

STEP 1 ▸ NEVER ASK TO BRING ANYTHING.

Much like a restaurant, the goal of a dinner party is ultimately to feed people. That responsibility lies squarely on the shoulders of the people who sent out the invites. If you are asked to bring something, just decline. The worst that could happen is they will rescind the invite. Actually, that is the best thing that could happen.

STEP 2 ▸ FIND THE GOOD BOOZE.

The hosts want you to think they've taken out all their best bubbly for the occasion. Not even close. Check the liquor cabinet. There is probably a forty-year-old bottle of Scotch on the shelf saved for a special occasion, or anything better than the bottom-shelf booze they are passing around. Ask the host why he/she is holding out on the party by keeping the good stuff locked up in the cabinet.

STEP 3 ▸ DOMINATE THE EVENING.

Dinner parties usually suck because the hosts are the
catalyst for the event but they are too busy playing host
to realize everyone is actually bored turdless. A true asshole will move everything along. Simple questions will
suffice: "When is the main course?" "What's for dessert?" "Should we throw our partners in the middle of
the room and play a fun game of swingers?" Keep the
party moving.

STEP 4 ▸ THE NIGHT IS OVER WHEN YOU WANT IT TO BE OVER.

There is nothing worse than a party that drags on
because no one wants to be the first person to leave, so
it's in your best interest to be the first to scram. A good
rule of thumb is to leave whenever the hell you feel like
it. "I'd love to wait around but I've got places to go and
people to do. Post the highlights on YouTube for me."
Also, take a dinner roll and a drink for the road. It's a
long cab ride to the bar.

Chapter 2.
Dealing with Family

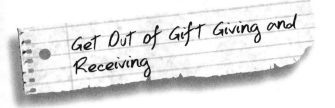

Get Out of Gift Giving and Receiving

Family can be a drain. Not just mentally, but financially. Especially for special occasions like the holidays, birthdays, and weddings. It seems like every other month you're forking out money for a gift to send to a cousin you never see or an aunt you haven't talked to since she got drunk at your high-school graduation. Pile on the fact that when your birthday or a holiday does roll around, they spare no expense to get you all the nice tchotchkes the dollar store has to offer. Monkey salt shakers! You shouldn't have! Honestly, you shouldn't have, and I said the same thing last year when you gave them to me for my birthday.

The Problem
You're handing out gifts and cash and getting nothing in return from ungrateful relatives. The buck stops here. Well it actually stops in your wallet.

The 'Hole Truth
It's easy to stop the freebies to distant kin. It's also just as easy to stop them from gifting you crap. You've just got to accept the fact that things could get a little uncomfortable the first few times. I'm sure you're fine with that, unless you could use another hand towel warmer. It did come in handy, um, never.

OPTION 1 ► LAY THE GROUNDWORK FOR "MONEY ISSUES."

A few months before a special event, drop subtle hints that money is tight and you're barely scraping by each month. Only a bunch of douche bags would expect gifts from a person having financial issues.

OPTION 2 ► A GIFT IN THEIR NAME.

Sort of. Donating money to charity in a person's name is all the rage. Especially because the recipient never really checks to see if money was indeed donated (frankly because they are pissed that some poor kid got their money/gift). Make up nice little cards that tell people you donated money to (make up fake charity here) in their name. Of course, you didn't donate anything but your time to make up those cards. Time well spent.

OPTION 3 ► THE JEDI GIFT TRICK.

This one is tough to pull off but could work out to your advantage over time. Instead of spending little or no money on their gifts, go nuts and buy them a ridiculously expensive present. It will embarrass the hell out of them, especially when you open the warm turds they bought as a gift. Thinking they could never top your generous gift, they might stop giving you gifts altogether, or even better, will feel obligated to return the favor and blow a ton of money on your next birthday or holiday.

OPTION 4 ► QUIT COLD TURKEY.

Just don't show up or send gifts. If they got something for you, thank them, but tell them again they really shouldn't have. Keep showing up without gifts even if you know they've got something for you. Eventually, after blowing dollar after dollar and getting nothing in return, they will get the hint.

DON'T BE A DOUCHE

Never complain about a gift to the giver, no matter how much it sucks. Some people are just terrible at buying gifts, which is one of the reasons places like Things Remembered and Vermont Teddy Bear stay in business. It's the thought that counts, even though they didn't put much into it.

Your little sister is all grown up and very attractive (not as attractive as her big brother, but not shabby). You've caught guys eyeing her up at the mall or in the gym. This is karma because of all the bad things you've done to women over the years. The Lord is a spiteful chap.

The Problem

She is seeing someone seriously and from the few times you've met him, he seems like a genuinely decent guy. She seems to really like him and he seems to feel the same. You like the dude. That doesn't mean you're not going to screw with his head for a little while just to show who is in control.

The 'Hole Truth

You're family, and blood, so you're allowed to act like a prick to anyone outside the family. You just can't do it alone. You've got to get the whole family involved. Here are some steps to follow.

STEP 1 ▸ GET HIM ALONE.

If you try screwing with him while your sister is around she is going to call your bluff. Get him alone and really lay it on thick. Do something weird like sharpen a knife or cut down a tree using only a butter knife and one hand. Don't let the conversation have a flow—talk about random things until he is incredibly confused. Every few cuts, remove the butter knife from the tree and lick it.

STEP 2 ▸ BLOW YOUR STACK ONCE, FOR NO GOOD REASON.

Just make sure he is around to see it happen. You are fixing something around the house or a car goes speeding past the house. Jump up and start screaming expletives and get incredibly red in the face. Go into heavy breathing through your mouth in a spit/breathing type of move. Then sit down and pretend nothing happened.

STEP 3 ▸ PAY HER FRIENDS TO SAY WHAT A BADASS YOU ARE.

You know those girls that are always hanging in your house, eating your food and making you wish you were a couple years younger? They need money to buy those washcloths they refer to as clothing. Throw them a couple of bucks to whisper in this kid's ear that you're very overprotective and that they have seen you flip out on some of your sister's ex-boyfriends. The more over-the-top they get, the more you pay up.

STEP 4 ▸ MAKE IT OBVIOUS YOU'RE STALKING HIM.

Bump into him at the store. Bump into him at the mall. Accidentally run into each other at the Justin Bieber concert. Show him you're following his every move and if he slips up, or cheats on your sister, or does anything you find questionable, you'll string him up by his sideburns and let raccoons feast on his balls.

⊣ DON'T BE A DOUCHE ⊢

If you want your sister to continue speaking to you, keep up the game just for a little while; otherwise, you risk veering into douche territory. . . .

Never Lift a Finger Around the House

In your teens you were expected to help out around the house. You obliged because you didn't pay the bills and your parents had the power to make your life hell. You moved out and eventually shacked up with a special someone who thinks having a man around the house is just as good as a having a servant.

The Problem

Your girl expects you to help out. Apparently paying for the place isn't good enough. You've got better things to do than pull weeds, build bookshelves, and paint a new room each month according to her whims.

The 'Hole Truth

As much as she likes to go on about home maintenance being part of your responsibility, you're only really responsible for seeing that it all gets done. The means to that end are totally up to you. Here are four options for getting things accomplished without lifting a finger.

OPTION 1 ▸ FIND A JACK-OF-ALL-TRADES.

There has to be at least one guy in your circle of friends who is good at just about everything from building and electrical to plumbing and minor repairs. The guy who spends his free time giving himself home improvement projects to work on. Right! That jackass. Get him to fix everything and pay him for the service. Actually, just keep him on a retainer.

⊦ DON'T BE A DOUCHE ⊦

Pay the guy a respectable wage. He is doing things you can't/won't do and saving you time. Make it worth his while.

OPTION 2 ▸ KEEP SCREWING IT UP UNTIL SHE STOPS ASKING.

She has asked you to fix the garbage disposal a handful of times, and you totally would, if you knew what the fuck you were doing. Actually, you do know what you're doing, but if you fix this one thing she will just make you move on to the next, so it's best to screw it up every time you try. Make the situation worse by breaking it almost beyond repair so a simple fix becomes a huge ordeal. She'll never again ask you to touch anything around the house out of fear it will make matters worse.

OPTION 3 ▸ GET RID OF THE PROBLEM.

She hates the way the garage door squeaks? Just buy another garage door. The wet towels in the bathroom have been piling up for weeks? Just throw them out and buy new towels. Her check-engine light popped on? It's probably best to light the entire car on fire and buy a new one. Don't fix—just dispose of the problem.

OPTION 4 ▸ CANCEL YOUR CABLE.

It's cable stations like HGTV and TLC that make it seem like anyone with a hammer and free weekend can make huge renovations or repairs to a house with minimal effort. It's hard not to get influenced when she watches TV every waking moment of the day. Cancel those stations. Better yet, cancel all cable and just watch TV online. If she complains, put a mallet through the TV and tell her you'll get around to fixing it eventually.

Your Brother Just Beat You: Show Him Who's Boss

Over the years you've dominated your siblings in almost every part of life. You were better in school, better in sports, better in life, and it was obvious to all that you were the best of the sibling bunch. Occasionally, luck strikes and one of your brothers does something just a little better. This isn't acceptable.

The Problem

Your brother just beat you at something you normally dominate: a video game, one-on-one, or maybe he just got a better job or a nicer car. You are clearly in second place in the situation. Everyone knows second place is the first loser. Wow, look at the way your first loser medal shines in the sunlight.

The 'Hole Truth

While there is no way to save face in the situation, there is a way to bring it down to a lower level and make him feel terrible about all the other things that went wrong in his life. Luckily, about a thousand different ideas spring to mind.

OPTION 1 ▸ REFUSE TO ADMIT DEFEAT.

Remember when you were kids and there were those off moments when he got the upper hand and came out on top but you had the smarts to throw a monkey wrench into the machine like changing the rules on the fly, refusing to acknowledge defeat, or just pretending it never happened? Those tricks still work, but the best part is they make him even angrier as an adult. It's one thing for a ten-year-old to pull that shit, but it's infuriating when a grown man says something didn't happen.

OPTION 2 ▸ RELATE THE VICTORY TO A RECENT LOSS.

Acknowledge his victory but let him know it's probably not going to do much to ease the pain of a recent heartbreaking event. "Good job beating me at air hockey. Too bad your ex-girlfriend that cheated on you with that hockey team wasn't here to see your victory. This is kinda like hockey. It might have loosened her legs for you too."

OPTION 3 ▸ EXPLAIN HIS PLACE IN THE FAMILY.

Every sibling has played the "mom and dad called you a mistake" card on the others. You need to explain that mom and dad told you long ago they expect only so much out of him and that anything he does above and beyond those expectations is a remarkable achievement. They have him pegged as one social level above a retard. Tell him some mistakes can be fixed, but there is no helping his lost cause. Drastic? Hell no, he just beat you at a round of golf.

OPTION 4 ▸ GET MOM AND DAD INVOLVED.

It's one thing to take shit from a brother, but it's a lot worse when mom and dad start chiming in and explaining in the nicest of ways how big of a loser and disappointment to the family he has become in just a short time. Oh, and get them to actually call him a mistake. MUCH worse.

┤ DON'T BE A DOUCHE ├

Nothing is won by an immediate "rematch," so save your time. The first victory always counts the most.

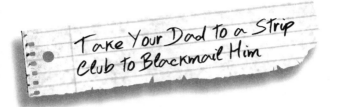

Take Your Dad To a Strip Club To Blackmail Him

Dad has been busting your balls for years. He was constantly the bad cop in the parental role-play game. You do love him, though, and he deserves a little reward. Wouldn't it be fun to take dad to a strip club when he wasn't expecting it? Wouldn't it also be fun to hold it over his head until he dies?

The Problem

Your dad embarrasses you in front of friends (especially women) with stories from your youth, before you knew better and weren't the smart and confident asshole you are today. You need something to hold over his head to keep him from flapping his gums. Mom is out of town and you invite him to go out to dinner. Your treat. You know a quiet little place with great food and really "hands on" service.

The 'Hole Truth

It's a strip club. He won't resist. He hasn't seen a new pair of tits in his face since he voted for Jimmy Carter. You've got to make sure he has a good time (for his sake) and it's all well documented (for your sake).

STEP 1 ▸ TAKE SOME PICTURES.

There is little chance dad is going to pose with a stripper so you've got to be sneaky and use your phone to capture all of the actions and candid shots. Oh man, look at the look on his face. He just got about ten years younger after one dance of Girls! Girls! Girls! That might make an awesome Christmas card.

STEP 2 ▸ BUY HIM LAP DANCES.

Your dad isn't going to know the strip club protocol and he probably isn't going to buy himself a dance, so you've got to fork over the cash to get some baby-oiled funbags in his face. First ask his opinion of which girl he likes the best and then get her to stick around and dance for a couple songs. Start snapping pics again!

STEP 3 ▸ GET HIM BUZZED.

Dad is a feisty old coot when he gets a couple Jack and Cokes running through his veins. Keep the drinks flowing and dad will loosen up more than his prostate did during last Monday's exam. He will start to buy his own dances, get his own girls over, and even stand up for a dance or two. He wants to know what a Champagne Room is. Isn't that adorable!

STEP 4 ▸ SHOW HIM WHAT A GREAT TIME HE HAD (THEN THREATEN TO SHOW MOM).

It's the next morning. Dad is still lit like a Christmas tree and needs help piecing together the events of the evening. Luckily you've printed them all out for a brag book he can show friends and even mom if he wanted. Oh, don't mention it to mom? Oh, okay, your lips are sealed. All it took was a couple hundred bucks, his favorite Mickey Mantle baseball card, and his new lawnmower. If only he knew what a fun time mom had when you took her to the male strip show.

Make it a classy joint. Don't take the old man to a strip club where the chicks have C-section scars bigger than their fake tits. Remember, he is your dad.

Her Family Finds Your Secret Stash

A man is allowed his secret stash; porn, sex toys, booze, and even drugs if he can handle himself accordingly and it's nothing too illegal. A man's home is his castle and sometimes you've got to hide some shit around the castle to get through a day.

The Problem
Your girl's family was nosing around on a recent stay-over, vacation, or any reason you've all got to live under one roof for longer than a day, and they found your secret stash.

The 'Hole Truth
You've got to do damage control fast. If they already hate you, they are going to use this to build a case. If they like you, they will never trust you again and will soon be looking to build a case. Here are your options for getting out of the jam.

OPTION 1 ▸ IT'S A GAG GIFT.

Explain that a friend has a birthday or bachelor party coming up and you were put in charge of buying the joke gifts to embarrass him at a party. He is also a huge fan of Big Bad Latino Ass and likes to watch them while popping prescription Percocet bought in your name. Well, how the hell do you watch Latino chick porn? Sober?

OPTION 2 ▸ IN THE NAME OF SCIENCE.

You're taking part in a medical/social experiment into how pornography, drug use, and sex toys affect the mind of the modern man. You're a couple weeks into the research and you've been jotting everything down in a journal. If they ask to see the journal, tell them it's against the rules of the experiment, plus the pages are stuck together and the writing is sloppy because you usually jot things down high as a skyscraper.

OPTION 3 ▸ IT BELONGS TO SOMEONE ELSE.

The oldest lie in the book, but you never know what people will believe. The whole stash belongs to a friend and you're holding on to it for him until he gets his life in order. Fine, that was a lie. It is actually their daughter's stash. You didn't want to say anything but now that the cat is out of the bag maybe you can all address the issue and get her the help she so desperately needs. Where is she now? Probably a whorehouse getting all cracked up! Try her cell phone.

OPTION 4 ▸ LET'S PARTY?

Yes, you watch porn. Yes, you do recreational drugs. Yes, you like a nice butt plug now and then. How about her parents? They kinky? They into some video pleasure? Does it hurt to ask? The damage is already done—

why not see if there is a chance to party? Oh shit, her dad is into butt plugs. This = awkward.

⊢ DON'T BE A DOUCHE ⊢

That booger-sugar and black tar will send you to an early grave. Stick to marijuana. The worst that stuff will do is trick you into thinking Phish is a talented and enjoyable band.

Dump Your Entire Family in Four Easy Steps

You can choose your mate, your friends, and even your neighbors and the people you work with, but unfortunately you can't pick your family. You can, however, pick the members of the family you choose to stay in touch with and those you want to cut the limbs out from under so they fall hard off the family tree.

The Problem

Your bloodline is filled with deadbeats, beat-offs, and more scum than a YMCA shower stall. They all seemed so normal when you were a kid, but so did collecting Archie comics and grinding up against your mattress to masturbate. It's getting to the point you can't even share a name with these stains of the Earth.

The 'Hole Truth

The immediate family is a little harder to shake, but the further away from the nuclear family they fall, the easier it is to cut all ties that bind. Here are four steps to speed up the process.

STEP 1 ▸ STOP INVITING THEM TO IMPORTANT EVENTS.

It would be much more fun to celebrate milestones and achievements without relatives creeping out your friends, and cousins hitting on your girl like it's singles night at the soup kitchen. If they don't get invitations to birthdays, anniversaries, and even simple backyard barbecues, they will soon get the hint they aren't welcome mingling with the rest of the clan.

STEP 2 ▸ GO UNDERGROUND.

Cut off all means of contact. From changing your cell phone number and e-mail address to deleting your Facebook page, there should be no way of them getting in contact with you for any reason. If it's possible, move and leave no forwarding address. If they do happen to find you, do it all over again but this time don't get a new cell, e-mail, or house. Roam the earth Bruce Banner style. "You wouldn't like me when I'm homeless."

STEP 3 ▸ DO SOMETHING TO SHAME THE NAME.

Look, it's only a matter of time before they do something (else) embarrassing for all the world to see (possibly on YouTube), so beat them to the punch and drag the family name through the mud. Make it something interesting like . . . um . . . any of the other entries in this book should work.

STEP 4 ▸ BANG A COUSIN.

Lord knows you've thought about it since you hit puberty because she is pretty damn hot (yeah, I'm not sure how she comes from the same gene pool either), but now you've got the perfect excuse. It's fine to bang a cousin; you just can't marry her and have kids, because that's just sick. It's also where the deformed babies come from. Although, three eyes could produce a hell of a baseball player.

DON'T BE A DOUCHE

Make it a female cousin. I just had to make sure I made that very clear. Although, a male cousin would get rid of your family . . . um . . . it's up to you.

Chapter 3.

Working Hard at Hardly Working

How to Score Any
Job Interview

An asshole isn't qualified for every job that exists. That doesn't matter. An asshole can get any job he wants; he just has to convince himself the job is attainable. When that doesn't work, it's time for some good old-fashioned resume fudging, underhanded networking, and the timeless art of telling white lies about past positions and qualifications.

The Problem

There is a job available. It's the job you want and would punch your own mother in the dentures to get. Two problems: you're unqualified and your mother could beat the shit out of you with one hand tied behind her back fat.

The 'Hole Truth

Any working grunt can climb his way into the CEO chair, but unless you spill hot frying grease on your lap and get half the fast-food chain in the settlement, you're not seeing the CEO unless you are delivering his lunch order. The job can still be yours if you learn how to master the art of making yourself look incredibly more important, efficient, and productive than your past work experience would indicate to the naked eye.

CHEAT 1 ▸ GET PROFESSIONAL HELP.

"Professional" means a person paid to make your resume sparkle. Don't ask your brother with the new

Mac program that wants to reformat your entire resume to look like a Boondocks comic. Do a search online for professional resume writers and have them beef up your resume by making all the menial tasks you're responsible for on the job sound like they are a step away from being the president of the company.

CHEAT 2 ▸ PLAY THE NAME GAME.

Get the name of the person in charge of hiring for the position and get acquainted with him in a hundred different ways. Find and connect with him on LinkedIn, Twitter, Facebook, MySpace, Friendster, Classmates, Dungeons and Dragons Fan Clubs, and join his weekend apple-picking club. Holy turds on rope, you love Gala apples? So do I!

Once you've initiated contact, slowly begin to introduce yourself through friendly banter and social comments. Respond to him on Twitter, Like his kids' pictures on Facebook, and slowly become an acquaintance. He will have no idea why he knows you or how you got connected, but for some reason your name and face seem very familiar now that you're swimming right next to each other at the same pool. You do laps here at 5 A.M. too? Jeez Louise that's coincidental! Man, I'm hungry after all this swimming. Wanna share my Gala apple?

CHEAT 3 ▸ IMPROVISE YOUR OWN REFERENCE.

This is where important friends come in handy, and an asshole tends to have plenty of those at his disposable. Get a high-ranking official in another company to call the company where you want to interview and put in a good word with the owner or person making the hiring decision. "Hello, Steve. This is Ted Tedderson from Apex. I saw this job listing you've got for head Brazilian waxer at the Kardashian house and I've got a guy I think would be perfect for the position. I'd love to hire him here but the son of a bitch might take my job one day, that's how smart and savvy the guy is. How did I know you were hiring? We must have a bad connection." CLICK.

CHEAT 4 ▶ CALL AND REQUEST AN INTERVIEW.

The ad says "no phone calls please," but if they really meant it why is it so easy to find the number? Just call the person hiring, state your case plain and simple, and explain that all you're asking for is an interview, even if it's just over the phone from the safety of his own office.

⊢ DON'T BE A DOUCHE ⊣

While there are many companies that people would die to work for, only a douche applies to every single position available.

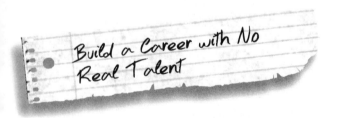

Build a Career with No Real Talent

This is the wonderful thing about the world today. An abundance of butter. Also pretty sweet is the fact you could have little skill, talent, or even brain power and still make a nice life for yourself.

The Problem

You need a path in life. Money too. More so money, because money makes the stripper go round. Did I say stripper? I meant world. Though it does make a stripper go round too. It will make a stripper do pretty much anything, especially that "bend over, trace her finger over the butt crack, then slap her cheek" move. Does anyone find that arousing? If you give her money, maybe she will stop doing that move. See, money does make the world go round. You need money and a career but have little talent. Time to improvise.

The 'Hole Truth

A career and tons of money are within your grasp. You've just got to be creative and ready to commit 100 percent of your time and energy to an activity that seems pretty fucking pointless to at least 95 percent of the population. It's paying attention to the other 5 percent that will make you rich and important.

STEP 1 ▸ FIND SOMETHING YOU'RE GOOD AT AND BECOME THE BEST AT IT.

It doesn't matter. Fishing, cutting shrubs, beer pong, or Battleship—just find a niche and become a master at its craft. For this example, let's take the yo-yo. Normally, the easier the skill the better, because people will think "hell, I can do that too," and they can, but just not as good as you. You can walk the dog, but can you do man on a flying trapeze? Do you even know what those terms mean? Amateur. This will make them feel inferior and look up to you as an example or authority.

STEP 2 ▸ CONVINCE PEOPLE IT'S A SKILL THAT EVERYONE SHOULD LEARN.

You can do this through word of mouth, at parties, family gatherings, or even at work. If you're fantastic at yo-yo tricks you must convince everyone you meet that they too can be just as wonderful at yo-yo tricks if they just take the time to practice. You have them right where you want them, so it's time to go in to skin the cat. (Note: Skin the cat is a yo-yo term. It's another way of saying "go in for the kill." Do not skin a cat. The last thing I need is PETA on my ass. Although, the attention might help book sales. Can you skin a cat with a yo-yo?)

STEP 3 ▸ CHARGE PEOPLE OBSCENE AMOUNTS OF MONEY TO LEARN.

So you want to learn yo-yo? Of course you do. Who doesn't? Just send $99.99 to this address and I'll send the twenty-minute instructional video "Yo-Yo Ma Look! I'm Good at Yo-Yo!" and a personalized yo-yo for practicing. People will pay this much money. I have no idea why. Infomercials and the popularity of the shitty items they sell is beyond my realm of understanding. Half the world is walking around wearing backwards bathrobes to keep warm. It mystifies me to this day.

STEP 4 ▸ TAKE TO THE INTERNET.

Just a few years ago an asshole's sphere of influence was limited. The Internet now allows any normal person to become a superstar with little or no real talent. All you need are social networking accounts like Twitter and Facebook and a couple bucks to pay a company to push followers your way. The next thing you know you're doing yo-yo demonstrations on the *Today* show and starting on a national tour with opening act Gallagher. The *Today* show appearance went well but Hoda Kotb kind of gave you the cold shoulder. Serves you right, you did piss on her calico.

⊣ DON'T BE A DOUCHE ⊢

Assholes who succeed on little talent accept one fact: they really don't have a talent; they are just extremely lucky. A douche drinks his own Kool-Aid and thinks he is the most amazing, versatile, talented, and ingenious person in the world. Looking right at ya Jamie Foxx.

Fire Your Close Friend

There is a reason you've reached such a prestigious position within the company. You handle shit. No situation too big or too small. You've just been given a small task by your boss that could turn into a major catastrophe if it isn't handled with kid gloves. He wants you to fire your best friend at work.

The Problem

While business is never personal, this isn't exactly cutting loose the account rep that spends his afternoons browsing Adult Friend Finder and downloading Aqua *Teen Hunger Force* episodes to watch, well, all day. This is a close friend. This is going to metaphorically sting—unless he launches a haymaker right at your lips. Then it's going to actually hurt.

The 'Hole Truth

In the first book I discussed the difference between real friends at work and cofriends (those people you consider friends just because you spend eight hours a day in their company). Figure which this guy really is and plan accordingly. If he is just a cofriend, cut his ass loose. If he is an actual friend, take these steps to ensure he gets let go as easily as possible and you retain all your teeth.

STEP 1 ▸ GIVE HIM AN IMPOSSIBLE TASK.

Make it an assignment you know there is no way in hell he could ever accomplish without a divine miracle. Stress how important this assignment is and that you, along with everyone else in management, is counting on him. Chances are he will fuck it up royally and will admit as much. It will all be a slippery slope from there and a failure he will carry into each new task he is assigned. It will also be easier to justify his eventual pink slip with such a big failure hanging over his head.

STEP 2 ▸ START A RUMOR HE IS GETTING FIRED.

Ever notice that you usually know who is getting fired in your company before they even have a clue? Think that is the work of a common asshole? Nope. It's an asshole from up above laying the groundwork so when it does go down no one is shocked. This rumor sets in motion two possible courses of action for the person on the chopping block. The first is that he gets wind of the rumor and starts interviewing for other jobs so he can have the satisfaction of quitting before he gets fired. The other possibility is he waits to get the ax, files for unemployment, and comes back with a homemade explosive device strapped to his side. Let's hope for the second outcome, because then at least the company will get a new office out of the ordeal. Just kidding. I don't condone going postal. On the plus side, you're friends, so he might wait for the day you call in sick. More vacation time for you!

STEP 3 ▸ WAIT UNTIL HE IS HAVING A GREAT DAY.

Ever have one of those days where it seems like nothing can go wrong? Even the smallest little details go better than expected, like you catch every green light on the way to work and it turns out your mistress is indeed just getting fat and is not pregnant. It's just an all-around fantastical day and even when something does go wrong, and it has to because life ain't all cherry blossoms and rub-and-tugs and you normally don't mind because the rest of the day has gone so well. Yup. Wait for the guy to have that day. You're gonna know because he is your friend and he will want to share. Wait until he is done, then tell him flat-out he is fired but at least he didn't hit traffic on the way to the office.

STEP 4 ▸ TAKE HIM OUT AND GET HIM WASTED (IF HE HASN'T PUNCHED YOU IN THE FACE YET).

Just give it to him straight. You are friends and he will understand, plus he probably realizes this isn't your decision. You're just doing what you've been asked to do. Actually, instead of taking him out for drinks after, take him to drinks during the canning. Then get him blasted on the company Amex. It's the least you can do, asshole.

DON'T BE A DOUCHE

Let him leave with some dignity. Unless you think he is gonna torch the place or spread a virus throughout the company worse than that freshman chick did to your entire dorm in college, let him gather his belongings and get some info off his computer before he leaves the office. If an escort is company protocol, save the rent-a-cops and escort him to his car yourself. Just be careful. Getting run over hurts a little more than a punch to the face.

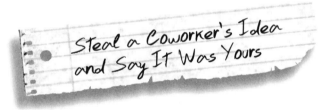

Steal a Coworker's Idea and Say It Was Yours

Great ideas only come around once in a lifetime. Even assholes fail a good portion of the time. Aside from great ideas, there are occasionally those fantastic ideas that change the way people live, work, and survive. Some good examples would be the invention of fire and the TV show *Web Soup*. An asshole always has great ideas, but the fantastic ideas might not come as easy.

The Problem

Your underlings are making you look bad in meetings because they've got better ideas that will help the company and its bottom line. Sure, it's nice that everyone is pitching in, but if you don't start hatching some killer ideas, those underneath you could soon be working from above in a much better position.

The 'Hole Truth

Until you come up with something of your own, it's time to start calling some of those ideas your own. This will have to be done without coworkers realizing you are taking credit for their brilliance. In other words, you've got to be a sneaky and creative asshole.

OPTION 1 ▸ THE BRAINSTORMING MEETINGS.

These can be held either with the entire staff or one-on-one. Try to make it a monthly occurrence but don't make it obvious that any of the ideas used in the meetings will be implemented right away. Make it seem like you're just "taking the pulse" of the staff and getting an idea of what works and what doesn't with company procedure. Even if they don't offer up anything to take to the big bosses, it might help spark some ideas of your own. That's why it's called brainstorming. Your brain gets involved too.

OPTION 2 ▸ THE "OTHER COMPANY" QUESTIONS.

This normally works best when dealing with staff that recently came over from another company or previously worked with a larger company before joining the firm. Ask how they did things at their old place of work. How did they handle situations X, Y, and Z? In this case you're not even stealing his or her idea, just the knowledge they possess as it relates to other companies.

OPTION 3 ▸ THE CASUAL LUNCH.

Take her out to lunch but barely discuss work. Ask her a ton of questions that will get her mind off the fact that for eight hours a day you share a boss/worker relationship. Once she gets really comfortable spilling her guts, ask her about ideas in regard to the office. After she fesses up that she hasn't had sex in months or that she's got zero cash in the bank but her partner is clueless, she will have no problem sharing work information. Might also be a good time to get any possible office gossip. Or sleep with her. Come on, she said months. It should be simple to seal that deal.

OPTION 4 ▸ JUST STEAL THE IDEA.

If a person you're mining for ideas complains to the higher-ups, it's your word against his and besides, in the end a company really doesn't give a crap where the idea originates so long as it makes things better and saves them money. Of course, now you've got another enemy on your hands, but this isn't a popularity contest.

┤ DON'T BE A DOUCHE ├

Don't make this a habit. Word will travel around the office that you're a douche who doesn't have any of his own good ideas, and people will be hesitant to talk to you about anything work-related.

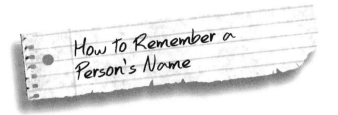

How To Remember a Person's Name

Remembering names is a vital trait for getting ahead in business. It makes people feel like you were paying attention when they talked and cared enough about the interaction to remember every detail. It makes them feel special. Don't you want everyone to feel special? Just not in a "friendly uncle" kind of way.

The Problem

You've just met an important business contact. He said his name in the first few minutes of the conversation, but that was twenty minutes and two martinis ago. His name had something to do with a month. August? Groundhog Day?

The 'Hole Truth

Remembering names is as easy as remembering the lines to your favorite movie or song. You memorized those word for word. Here are some simple ways to remember a person's name and some tricks to get him to say it again.

STEP 1 ▸ AS SOON AS HE SAYS HIS NAME, REPEAT IT.

If you know you forget names, pay close attention to the conversation and wait until he says his name. Then repeat it back like you're deaf. "Skip?" "Yes, Skip?" "Okay, Skip—that's an easy name to remember." You've now said and heard it a few times. Yes, it's an awful name, but you're just here to remember, not judge.

STEP 2 ▸ USE HIS NAME OVER AND OVER.

It's annoying as hell and usually a tactic of shady salespeople, but using a person's name tons of times in a normal conversation is an easy way to meld the name into your brain. "Skip—I'm going to tell you something, Skip. The last time I had a margarita this delicious, Skip, I ended up being pantless and on stage lip-synching 'I'm Every Woman' along with the incomparable Whitney Houston. Want another drink, Skip?"

STEP 3 ▸ ASK FOR A BUSINESS CARD.

It's a name in a pocket. You'll have to make up some lame excuse about why you'd actually want a business card at a backyard BBQ, but then every time you forget the name, just pull it out and take a peek. Pull out the BUSINESS CARD! Zip your pants back up. If there is a chance of meeting again, jot down some reminders about the encounter when you get home. "Skip. Met at Steve's BBQ. Smelled of hot dogs and Ben-Gay ointment."

STEP 4 ▸ INTRODUCE HIM TO SOMEONE ELSE.

It's the easiest way to get him to say his name again. Drag someone into the conversation and introduce only the new person. This will get the mystery man to give his name again one more time. Awesome. Now if you can't remember, you can ask the other person, and then at least there will be two people who can't remember his name.

If none of the above seems to be working, try these odd tactics.

OPTION 1 ▸ PUT IT IN A SONG OR RHYME.

It works for poison ivy, the days in the month, and what do to with a woman's vagina (If it smells like fish, eat all you wish, if it smells like cologne, leave it alone!), so why not try it to remember names? "Skip, Skip, what a dip. Met him at a BBQ, waiting for the burgers to flip." It works. Just make sure you don't confuse his name for Flip.

OPTION 2 ▸ PRETEND IT'S AN ODD NAME (EVEN IF YOU'VE HEARD IT A LOT).

After he says his name, ask a hundred questions like it's the most exotic and original name you've ever heard, even if it's older than your mother's bachelorette party vibrator. "Skip? Is that a family name? It's different. Never heard of Skip. Did your parents make that up? Were they homosexuals? Was the second runner-up name Sashay?"

DON'T BE A DOUCHE

You are allowed one "what's your name again?" question per person. Never ask the same person that question twice. If you can't remember his name after the first time he reminds you, you deserve to be a called a douche.

Visit the Office Fridge for Free Food

You ran out of house this morning (you just weren't ready to say goodbye to Ms. Last Night) and forgot to grab some food to get you through the day. It's hours until you can leave to grab lunch, and the office vending machine is stocked full of Chuckles and little else. The office fridge, however, is a regular buffet of tasty snacks that will stop the stomach rumbles in no time.

The Problem

Sure it's a dick move taking another person's food, but it's even worse to pass out from starvation. Fine, you're not going to starve, but you've got that nauseous sensation in your gut and it's making it impossible to concentrate on work. You got to eat something that unfortunately belongs to someone else. You just have to be careful to not get caught. No asshole wants to get fired over a bag of Sun Chips.

The 'Hole Truth

If you remember Demandment I—The asshole cares about the asshole the most—it will be easier to just take what you want without feeling guilt or remorse. Here are a few simple steps for snagging some tasty vittles from the office fridge without anyone knowing (well, not until lunch).

STEP 1 ▸ WAIT UNTIL 9:30 A.M.

By this time, everyone is usually at work so no one will be walking into the kitchen to put their lunch in the fridge and you'll have a much bigger selection from which to choose. It's also less likely anyone will come in looking for food because breakfast wasn't that long ago. You'll be all alone with the defenseless grocery bags of goodness.

STEP 2 ▸ TAKE FROM THE FRONT FIRST.

The lunches up front are from the people who got to work last. They are the least likely to come back looking for their food at an earlier hour. This decreases your chances of getting caught but also increases the suspect list because everyone will head to the fridge before them to grab lunch.

STEP 3 ▸ STICK TO AFTERNOON SNACKS.

People obviously pack according to meals. Foods like fruit, yogurt, and oatmeal are morning fare, while after-lunch snacks are of the chips and nuts variety. Grab the obvious afternoon snacks. When a person comes back to grab her morning snack she might not even notice the other stuff is gone or might just assume she forgot to pack it.

STEP 4 ▸ JUST TAKE THE WHOLE DAMN THING.

If you take only a snack or even just a sandwich it looks like a personal attack and less like an honest mistake. If you just take the whole damn lunch it looks like someone was a moron and grabbed the wrong bag. It will likely set off a chain reaction of people taking each other's lunches out of spite. It will be anarchy! Get your hands of my banana!

┤ DON'T BE A DOUCHE ├

Take the whole snack. Don't be a douche and take handfuls of food or sips of a drink. It's disgusting and really throwing it in a coworker's face that you've just stolen from her.

Get the Boss to Dish the Dirt

Those in positions of authority are usually pretty tight-lipped. They have a small group of advisers in which they confide but never discuss business practices with people outside the circle of trust. You need to get inside that circle. For your own career advancement, you've got to have insider info about the company so you can act accordingly.

The Problem

How do you get in the boss's inner circle without looking like an ass-kissing douche? And once you've become a part of the circle, how do you get him to start yapping like a high-school broad in a guidance counselor's office? You want to be the first to know when shit hits the fan—unless you just wait for the eventual stink. Also, you might want to get to the bottom of who is flinging poo at the fan. This isn't a fraternity. It's a place of business.

The 'Hole Truth

The boss is hard to get close to, and it's not just because of his pharmacy-brand cologne. He doesn't usually make friendly with his staff, but if you keep trying he eventually will crack (if only for the reason that you'll stop asking). If at first you don't succeed, try, try again. Then try again with football tickets.

STEP 1 ▸ GET CLOSER IN THE OFFICE.

This isn't really that hard and only involves a couple well-timed drop-ins to his office. The two best times to knock on his door with a question are just before lunch or after a huge meeting. If he is still at his desk between the hours of 12 and 1 P.M., stop in to ask him a question and then casually ask if he wants to grab some food. You're on your way out and figured you'd ask. If he just emerged from a big meeting that you weren't involved in, drop by his office to discuss something totally unrelated. Before you leave, ask him if everything went okay, because he seems stressed. He will either confide or tell you to butt the hell out.

STEP 2 ▸ GET CLOSER OUTSIDE THE OFFICE.

All those instances when you could use an extra guy (poker night, golf outing, or bus trip to a Rub-n-Tug massage parlor) are good chances to invite the boss for some extracurricular fun. Especially if the offer is a freebie (free tickets, free entry, or free happy ending), because no one likes to get invited places and have to pay. It makes a person feel like an afterthought with a charge card.

STEP 3 ▸ SHARE INFO FIRST.

If he has rebuffed your advances of lunchtime pow-wows and after-hours trips to the strip club (this is harder than dating!), it's time to keep it just business. Keep it all business and confide in him first. Any business decision you had to make that he might not be aware of, whether it was dealing with a client or a coworker, tell him all about it and how you handled it. He might reciprocate and dish the dirt about some of the things he is dealing with.

STEP 4 ▸ RAT SOMEONE OUT.

It's a dick move, borderline douchey, but it's for the greater good. In this case, your career is the greater good. People like to know who is loyal and who is out for himself. Pick on a low man on the totem pole and throw him under the bus for something the boss would consider insubordination. Just don't get the guy fired. Unless he's a douche; then it's fine.

DON'T BE A DOUCHE

No one likes an ass-kissing douche. You know what I am talking about.

Wooderson opined in the movie *Dazed and Confused* that the thing he loved most about high-school girls is that even though he grew older, they always stayed the same age. Much the same can be said about the fresh batch of interns that arrive at the office every semester. In this instance, all of the interns are of legal age and you'd like nothing more than to stick your USB plug into that long-legged one's port.

The Problem

You're a couple lunches away from taking an intern out to your car and showing her what this business is all about. It's not the business she is earning college credits for, but it will be an education. It will be fun for about two weeks and then she will get attached, you'll get bored, and it will all get very awkward.

The 'Hole Truth

You can't have her making a scene in the office or going to management about the whole affair. She is young, volatile, and honestly doesn't give a shit about your career or this internship, so she will be more than happy to screw you over. You've got to lay her and then get her fired.

STEP 1 ▸ NOTICE THAT "THINGS ARE GOING MISSING" AROUND THE OFFICE.

First it's little things like supplies, laptop computers, and desk chairs, but then it's major items like petty cash and the owner's car. It all started with the new crop of interns. You're speculating it's the good-looking one with the nice ass that has a small mole on the left cheek. She looks like a kleptomaniac. Also looks like a cutter. She might also like it when you pull her hair and call her "hooker." Again, all just speculation.

STEP 2 ▸ PLANT SAID "MISSING ITEMS" IN HER PURSE.

Hang out near her during lunch and when she gets up for a package of Chuckles from the vending machine put some of the office supplies in her purse. Don't worry, she won't notice, because that thing is the size of a mother-humping feedbag and it's got more junk in it than Fred Sanford's pickup.

STEP 3 ▸ HAVE SOMEONE ELSE CATCH HER.

When you get back from lunch, mention to the office gossip that you went to lunch with Hooker . . . er, Emily. You went to lunch with Emily and think you saw the new office projector in her purse. If your first choice doesn't bite, go to the boss or Human Resources. Just try to distance yourself and ask to be left out of the whole ordeal.

STEP 4 ▸ START BANGING HER AGAIN.

After she is let go from the job and loses all the credits for college, feel free to start sleeping with her again. She doesn't work there anymore and hates the place, so won't ever want to discuss it or talk about it at all. Just try to do it off company property. Meet her at local shopping center parking lot. I bet she'd love it, that dirty little hooker.

┤ DON'T BE A DOUCHE ├

Don't do this every semester. Take one or two off in between. Unless an incredibly hot chick starts interning. Well, all right, all right, all right.

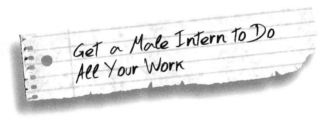

Get a Male Intern To Do All Your Work

Now that you're done pumping and dumping the female intern and spending your whole day formulating ways to get her fired, you've got a pile of work on your desk as high as Willie Nelson on his tour bus. Time to take one of the male interns under your wing and teach him what exactly you do around the office (honestly, everyone is curious). Then you get him to do that job for you.

The Problem

You'd be much more productive if it weren't for all this busywork associated with the position. (What was it again? Christ, that sounds made up.) If you just got all of it cleared off your plate, you could concentrate on all the big-ticket projects. This is why internships were created. Free and dumb labor.

The 'Hole Truth

He won't do a good job if he realizes he is doing all the crap you don't feel like finishing. You've got to make it seem like you're letting him do some of the most important work since the creation of the pacemaker. Trick him into thinking he is learning everything that will catapult him to a huge job after graduation. Yup kid, you'll be a CEO in no time once you master the incredibly difficult expense sheet. Here are other ways to keep him doing your grunt work.

STEP 1 ▸ COMMEND HIM ON SOMETHING A BLIND MONKEY COULD ACCOMPLISH.

You had the kid licking envelopes all afternoon. It was borderline torture. He hated it and hates you for it but that was before you tell him how impressed the boss was with his efforts and how one of those envelopes went to a huge client that is interested in doing business because the envelope was so well labeled and stayed sealed. He could be responsible for making the company millions. Butter his ego a bit.

STEP 2 ▸ TELL HIM HE IS DOING THE "ONLY GOOD PART OF THE JOB."

Make it seem like you'd really like to be doing the part of the job he is doing but you're too busy taking boring clients to lunch and holding meetings about major company acquisitions. You'd much rather be in the office going over reports and spreadsheets and filing all the great work you've accomplished. If he buys it, you certainly didn't pick the smartest intern.

STEP 3 ▸ THROW HIM A BONE.

A little reward once in a while doesn't hurt the working mule. Buy him lunch, get him a gift card to buy coffee, or let him take home all the stuff you planted on the intern that got fired. Okay, strike that last line from the record.

STEP 4 ▸ PUT IN A GOOD WORD.

Let the lackey know that once his internship is complete and it comes time for the boss to fill out the final evaluation, you'll be sure to tell him what an impressive young man the intern became and not only did he deserve full credit and the highest grade possible, he should get extra credits coming to him during the coming year. Hopefully the intern doesn't realize there is no such thing as a better-than-good evaluation and it's either pass/fail.

┤ DON'T BE A DOUCHE ├

It's difficult to commit these peons to memory, but if you're going to dump your shit work on him, at the very least, try to get his name right.

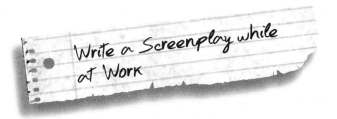

Write a Screenplay while at Work

Work is probably the best place to get things accomplished—things other than actual work. You can pay bills, make phone calls, search and shop online, and do all the things you don't have time to do when you're home. It's also a great time to work on that movie idea you've been talking about since high school. Let's see if you've got the chops.

The Problem

While work is a good eight hours of time, it does have more than its fair share of distractions, including a boss, coworkers, and the chick in the short skirt bending over at the fax just because she knows you are watching her closely. If you're serious about getting this movie written, you've got to avoid the distractions while making the most of the amenities and inspiration all around.

The 'Hole Truth

Joanne "Jo" Murray lost her gig as a secretary when she was caught writing creative stories on her work computer. You probably know her better as J. K. Rowling, author of the Harry Potter books. Calm down, dork. Anyway, it's just proof that working on other things during work can lead to you being a billionaire chick writer. Well, you know what I mean. This is what you've got to do.

STEP 1 ▸ DOWNLOAD SCRIPTWRITING SOFTWARE.

Writing a script is much easier when you've got the software. Much of it is very expensive and not worth the cash. That's why you're not paying for it. You're finding it on a pirated website and downloading it to your work computer. At least it's not as bad as porn.

STEP 2 ▸ USE COWORKERS AS INSPIRATION.

Just look around at the people in your office. You couldn't write characters like these if you tried. The accountant who talks to his zipper. The woman who carries around a small tin of cheese in case of emergencies. It's writing gold. Call the most interesting people into your office and take notes for character studies. You can even record the conversations for playback at another time. Well, legally you can't, but you can if you don't get caught.

STEP 3 ▸ USE THE OFFICE SUPPLIES AVAILABLE.

Once the screenplay is complete, use the copier, fax, and free stamps to send it out to interested people. Obviously you need to make it look like actual office business, or someone is liable to get suspicious. "Why is Jim sending plumbing catalogs to Martin Scorsese?"

STEP 4 ▸ USE WORK TO SCHMOOZE PEOPLE TO HELP YOUR SCREENWRITING CAREER.

Getting into Hollywood takes a ton of time and a crapload of money. You've got the time, but it belongs to your company, so you've got to figure out how to balance both. You don't have the money, but you do have a business expense account and they never really check who you have lunch with so long as it's relatively cheap. Let's hope Scorsese has a small appetite.

Bail on a Company Event

After quitting time, the last people you want to hang out with are the coworkers who pissed you off for the last eight hours. More than a few companies are under the impression that people like hanging out outside the walls of the office. It's never the case.

The Problem
The boss is trying to put together a company function for people to bond outside of the office. You want no part of it. Nor should any smart asshole. You've got to come up with a legitimate excuse to get out of this and any future team-building exercises without ticking off the boss or putting yourself in the line of fire at work.

The 'Hole Truth
It's easier than you think to get out of these functions. It's just that you have to think much farther ahead and can't

make it look like you are bailing at the last minute. Start early and avoid often.

OPTION 1 ▸ LAY THE GROUNDWORK EARLY.

If the event has a set date, make it known early on you've got obligations that day and won't be able to attend. The first person to tell is the boss. Put it in an e-mail so he has a record. Then when he asks you about attending the function, you've got notes he can go back and check.

OPTION 2 ▸ HAVE "LAST-MINUTE" WORK RESPONSIBILITIES.

You'd love to make an event but you scheduled a last-minute meeting with a client across town and it could turn into drinks and dinner. You'll even be late for that because there is work on your desk piling up that needs finishing. And even before you get to all that, you wanted to vacuum and dust around the office and tinker around with the copy machine. Work, work, work! Busy, busy! Pick up and put down the phone and shuffle papers while conveying how busy you are and how you're not going to make the extracurricular activities.

OPTION 3 ▸ THE EMERGENCY.

This can be handled one of two ways; either have the emergency pop up in the middle of work, or right before the function starts. If it should happen while you're at work, make sure it's later in the day and that everyone in the office knows you're leaving for the day. If you try to pull it off at the event, do it in front of a large group of people, preferably the boss. "What? The roof of the house did what? Popped off? What the hell is a time travel vortex? The Four Horsemen are on my lawn? I just seeded! I'll be right there."

How an Asshole "Works" from Home

People are working from home more than ever before
thanks to the advent of the Internet, allowing instant contact with coworkers and clients. That and the fact that
companies can't afford to have an actual office anymore.
You're now allowed to work from home a couple days a
week. It's a sweet setup.

The Problem
If you thought you didn't feel like doing work in the
office, you really won't feel like doing anything while
lying in bed watching Regis and Kelly. Bet Kelly is a
firecracker in the sack. Bet the same thing about Regis.
You don't want to do work, but you need to show some
progress and keep in light contact with the boss and other
staff so he doesn't take back the privilege.

The 'Hole Truth

You can pretend to work from the comfort of your La-Z-Boy without doing a lick of work. You've just got to make it look like you're busy as hell, because the people back at the office are keeping tabs. Here are some tricks to make it seem like you're working harder at home than you even do in the office. All of these can be done in between naps and *Full House* reruns.

STEP 1 ▸ BE THE FIRST PERSON TO E-MAIL IN THE MORNING.

Make sure to hit all the important people with some type of correspondence early in the A.M. before they all get to the office. It shows you're up and out of bed, alert and already doing work while everyone else is stumbling in and sipping coffee in the kitchen.

┤ DON'T BE A DOUCHE ├

Make it a work-related e-mail, and not one of those ridiculous forwards that always seem to come early in the morning. Yes, we've all seen the People of Walmart, so no need to send every damn picture.

STEP 2 ▸ LEAVE MESSAGES WHEN YOU KNOW PEOPLE AREN'T AT THEIR DESKS.

Wait until around lunchtime to call coworkers. It will look like you're working through lunch, and it means they aren't there to answer the phone, so it will go to voice mail. Tell them to give you a call back at home when they get a chance. Then when they call, don't answer and don't return the call. E-mail them and tell them you "answered your own question" but thanks for reaching out so quickly.

STEP 3 ▸ GET A CHAT CLIENT.

Pick something universal like Gmail's chat function so people can get in contact with you while you are working remotely. Then they won't have to call or e-mail (even though you're ignoring both). Set the status to "busy" and use a bogus message like "knee deep in work right now."

STEP 4 ▸ BE THE LAST ONE TO CHECK OUT.

This is the same idea as the first step except you're sending e-mails when everyone is obviously gone for the day. When they come in the next morning, they are hit with the late-night and the early morning e-mails. Shit, dude, don't you take a break?

You Got Passed Up for a Promotion: Start a War

Not everything goes an asshole's way. He doesn't always get the girl, the gold, or the glory. Sometimes things come between an asshole and his ultimate goal. In this case, the thing an asshole didn't factor into the equation of his ascension up the company ladder was another coworker (possibly another asshole) climbing the ladder at the same time.

The Problem

The boss has made a decision, and the cushy, corporate, and killer-paying job goes to a person not named (add your name here). The civil thing to do would be to take it like a man and accept the fact. You will be civil. Just like the war. The battle begins and you've got to fire the first shot.

The 'Hole Truth

There is a good chance this course of action could get you fired. You've got to accept that as the ultimate outcome. If you can accept that fate, then it's time to go to war.

STEP 1 ▸ BUILD AN ARMY.

A commanding officer is only as good as his battalion. It's vital to assemble a team of people who feel you were the better choice for the position. The bigger and stronger the support group the better, so make nice with anyone who has any pull around the office. This might be harder if you've stolen everyone's ideas, thrown them under the bus, and fired most of your close friends in the office. Hindsight is 20/20, asshole.

STEP 2 ▸ NICELY TELL THE BOSS HE MADE A BONEHEAD CHOICE.

A boss never likes to hear he has made a mistake, but in this case, feel free to tell him he chose the wrong man for the job. Explain all the reasons you would have been a better choice. If you make a valid enough argument, he will have no choice but to agree. It's also good for him to know you're not exactly thrilled with the recent turn of events. If you go down without a fight, he will think not only that you've accepted the decision, but that you might be secretly looking to jump ship. Of course, you probably *are* looking to jump ship. HINT HINT—you should be looking to jump ship.

STEP 3 ▸ UNDERMINE THE NEW BOSS WHENEVER POSSIBLE.

Just because he is in charge doesn't mean you have to listen. You can just yes him to death to his face and completely ignore his wishes. The result could either be an ax (the kind that chops you from a job) or less responsibility, due to the fact he doesn't give you any more work you would have to avoid. Nice! More time to look for another job. HINT HINT—you should be looking for another job.

STEP 4 ▸ IT'S MUTINY!

Time to turn the whole office against the guy who took your position. Constantly make him look like the bad guy to the rest of the office. Every time something goes wrong or a decision is made that negatively affects the rest of the staff, point the finger at him as being the main cause for the issue. The office has to work a holiday—it's his fault. No one is getting their yearly bonus because he gave himself a raise. There will be no holiday party this year because he killed Santa. Spread false rumors about him. Make sure you find out about and document every single time he screws up. Jizz in his coffee maker (be sure it dries first before putting it back). Make his life at work a living hell. Actually, this might be why he was promoted over you; you're spending all your time seeking revenge.

┤ DON'T BE A DOUCHE ├

A douche whines and complains to the boss. An asshole states his case calmly, and if he doesn't get his way, unleashes hell.

Your New Job Blows:
Get Your Old Job Back

Everyone should look ahead to the next step in their career. Especially the assholes. Often a job offer comes along that seems to be too good to be true and an asshole jumps at the chance and jumps ship. Especially when he starts getting passed up for promotions. This new offer not only seemed too good to be true—it really was. Sadly, you learned that the hard way. The new ship has a ton of holes and is sinking faster than Kirstie Alley in a dunk tank.

The Problem

You can still taste the Best of Luck cake from the office going-away party on your tongue while you sit in your new office and wonder how you got duped into taking such a terrible job. You can't stay here and sink along with the S.S. *Minnow* and you can't take any time off to search and interview for another new job. You'll have to go crawling back. Brush your teeth first, though. You shouldn't really still taste cake.

The 'Hole Truth

You left your old gig only forty-eight hours ago, so there is a still a chance, however slim, that you can go back without crawling on your hands and knees. If you left on good terms and didn't burn any bridges, the job could once again be yours, but it's going to take some bald-faced lies. Here are a few options.

OPTION 1 ▸ TELL YOUR OLD COMPANY YOU GOT SCREWED.

Make up a lie that you showed up Monday for your new job and there was no new job. The guy you were supposed to replace never left and they just forgot to notify you about the retracted offer.

OPTION 2 ▸ ACT LIKE YOU NEVER LEFT.

The two weeks' notice, the signed letter of resignation, the going-away party were all just a figment of everyone's imagination. Now, who wants to hit up Dunkin' Donuts?!?

OPTION 3 ▸ CALL YOUR OLD BOSS AND BE HONEST.

You took the job because it was a career advance, but after less than a day of work you realize the place is one casual Friday away from chaos. Maybe your old boss doesn't have any prospects for your position, hasn't set up any interviews, and really isn't in the mood to train a new person to take your place. He might consider a return if he can't find a suitable replacement.

OPTION 4 ▸ AN ASSHOLE ALWAYS LANDS ON HIS FEET AND MAKES THE BEST OUT OF EVERY TERRIBLE SITUATION.

Give the new job one more chance, but play by your own rules. The worst they can do is fire you, and you'll collect unemployment until something better comes along. There is also T.G.I. Friday's, the mall, a paper route, or a hundred mind-numbing gigs that are better than working a job you hate. Even if your old company doesn't take you back, just quit and work any gig until you find something else. You'll probably make manager in no time. They don't get many applicants that can make correct change and have all their teeth.

DON'T BE A DOUCHE

If they don't take you back, take it like a man. You're the guy who left in the first place. Don't be a douche, badmouthing the company every chance you get.

How to Burn a Bridge

The new job sucked and you left not long after the welcome! e-mail. After a month of phones calls, e-mails, and muffin baskets, your old company refuses to take you back. They've found a replacement and are moving on. You wish you could do the same, but you feel there is a score to settle.

The Problem

You're still unemployed. It might be time to find a new career path, but not before you exact just a tasty morsel of revenge on the little cupcakes at your previous employer. No, not that company; the place you willingly left. Not the last job, the job before that. Well shit, if you can't keep it straight, how the hell can I?

The 'Hole Truth

While I normally don't condone burning a bridge (because in business, things can come back to chomp on your ass when you least expect it), in this case you should take out your frustration on the company you never would have left had they promoted you in the first place. Here is how to burn a bridge, asshole style.

STEP 1 ▸ TAKE OUT AN AD.

Honestly, newspapers are dying for advertisers. Look at your local newspaper. Two original stories and coupons for lube jobs. They'll let you say or write just about anything so long as you pay up front. Take a full-page ad about your old company and push people toward doing business with its competitors. Sign it "from an ex-employee." Also, take a cheap shot at Ziggy. Little bastard needs to be knocked off his high horse. If that doesn't work, talk to someone in the newsroom. Tip them off to something shady in the company.

STEP 2 ▸ START AN ANONYMOUS BLOG ABOUT THE COMPANY.

Sure, blogs are very 1999, but that doesn't mean people don't write them, read them, or pass them around. If you work in an industry with millions of potential readers, dishing the dirt about a "fictional" company might just find a huge audience. Imagine a blog from an insider at Lehman Brothers. Would have been huge. Hell, a blog about Einstein Bros. Bagels can be interesting depending on the material. Both companies did blow through a ton of dough. RIMSHOT! Make sure to change all the names to protect your ass more than theirs, and be sure to e-mail it to people within the company as well as newspapers, e-mail lists, Facebook friends, and websites like Reddit. Say hello to the Reddit Alien while you're there. Such an adorable and informative creature.

STEP 3 ▸ TIP OFF THE FEDS.

Every company does something illegal. If you were with them long enough, and held a high enough position, you know all about it. Make a little phone call to the authorities and tip them off to the shenanigans. Be sure to use the actual word "shenanigans" because it's a fun word that doesn't get its proper due. I find that to be pure malarkey. Really think this through because this move could send a bunch of people to jail. You included, if your name is on any of that paperwork.

⊣ DON'T BE A DOUCHE ⊢

Make sure everything you're saying is 100 percent truth. Don't make things up for the sake of sensationalism. Douches lie. That would make a funny T-shirt. Also, a funny T-shirt would be "Assholes finish first. Then fall asleep before she does." Trademarked.

Chapter 4.

The Opposite Sex

Bang Her Best Friends

You've gone on a few dates with a woman and it's not working out. She is a fantastic chick and you've sunk her battleship on more than one occasion, but it's all leading to another game called "The Friendship Tip." You'll stay in touch with her but only because she runs with a pack of foxes and you're looking to hunt down one in particular.

The Problem

She has many hot friends. You want to nail one, or seven. You've got to pull it off without looking like you're using her to get to them and without getting labeled by the group as "off limits."

The 'Hole Truth

Any chick in the group is attainable. You've just got to make it known there is nothing going on between you and your ex to get in the way.

STEP 1 ▸ HANG OUT WITH THE GROUP, EVEN AFTER YOU'VE TOLD YOUR EX YOU'RE NO LONGER INTERESTED IN DATING.

You just had "the talk" and let her down easy. She seems fine, so you suggest getting together sometime to stay on friendly terms. Invite her (and some of her friends) out for a happy hour or function. If that doesn't work, accidentally bump into the group at one of their hangouts. Talk to her first and show the group you're a good guy.

STEP 2 ▸ DON'T ZONE IN ON A TARGET TOO SOON.

The ex-girlfriend might be fine with the way things turned out, but if she sees you hitting on one of her friends too early, she'll pick you off in the middle of your flight pattern and gun you down to the target in private. Spread out the mingling and flirting among the entire group. Always go back and talk to her in between.

DON'T BE A DOUCHE

Only a douche would blow her off and then immediately ask about and hit on her friends.

STEP 3 ▸ MAKE CONTACT AT A LATER DATE.

If you've got one friend in mind, remember her name and try to find her online. Yes, it's kind of cyber-stalking, but if she thinks you're hot it's called "he is interested." Remember, it's only harassment if you're ugly. If you're into a bunch of her friends, connect to a couple of them online or just accidentally bump into the group another time. Preferably when the original conquest isn't around.

STEP 4 ▸ TALK HER UP AND TALK YOURSELF DOWN.

If her friends ask what happened, be sure to make it seem like she is perfection and you're just not the type of guy she is looking for right now. Women love to hear how wonderful their friends are and when a guy is admittedly an asshole. You'll score major points for cutting it off early and not stringing her along and playing games like all the other guys. You are a good guy. A nice guy. An available, nice, good guy . . . do you see where this is going, or do I really have to keep making it so obvious??

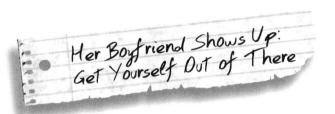

Her Boyfriend Shows Up:
Get Yourself Out of There

She was all over you at the bar and now you're all over her back at her apartment. You didn't pay too close attention, but there are several clues in the place that make it seem like she has a boyfriend. Framed pictures with a guy, men's sneakers by the door, and the dude staring at you from the bedroom door.

The Problem

She forgot to mention her boyfriend. Maybe she did mention it but you forgot after a couple hours and a couple beers. She might have mentioned his name. It's best not to ask her, or him, the name right at this moment.

The 'Hole Truth

You can talk your way out of this without having to punch your way out of it. He is angry right now but more at her, so use that to your advantage. Here are four options to help you walk out of there with minimal bruises.

OPTION 1 ▸ LOSE YOUR SHIT.

Go absolutely balls-to-the-wall nuts the moment he shows up. Pick up things around her place and start breaking them over your head. Grab food from the fridge and chuck it against the wall. Drink straight from the milk carton first, then masturbate into the little hole on top. Show him and her you're a wacko and they are better off if you just leave without more problems.

OPTION 2 ▸ PRETEND YOU KNOW HIM.

Act like you've met before. "Wow, Chuck, is that you? Small damn world. We worked together over at Citicom. I sat in the back office. Gene was my boss. Hey, you still working there? I talk to Gene once in a while over e-mail but I've lost touch with the rest of the staff. Is this your girlfriend? Crazy coincidence."

OPTION 3 ▸ SHIT YOUR PANTS.

Literally. Squeeze out a squirt right on her living-room rug. You've got a face-smashing coming anyway but at least you've got an interesting story to tell. "Yeah, so right before he punched my teeth down my gullet I dropped my lunch on her rug. It was priceless and I got a good look when I was laid out on the floor."

OPTION 4 ▸ I BELIEVE IT'S PRONOUNCED "MÉNAGE À TROIS."

They might be into the whole idea. This could end up being a very interesting night. Unless he finds you just as attractive as she does. Now it's time to shit your pants for an entirely different reason.

┤ DON'T BE A DOUCHE ├

Don't cry. Take the beating like a man. You never know, you might be able to take him. (Yeah, I chuckled at that notion too.)

Sex Was Great ... but She Is Still Here

You had a great time. Drinks were intoxicating, dinner was delicious, more drinks were an excellent idea, and sex on the hood of your car in the Arby's parking lot was a *Penthouse* letter in real life. A couple more glazings of her donut back at your place and you're ready to put on Adult Swim and sleep it all off.

The Problem

Well, it was a nice time. Yup. Nice time. Guess I'll call you soon. Oh, you're still in bed. Um, yeah, I guess you can stick around YAAAWNNNNNNNNNN but I'd really prefer if you didn't because . . . shit, she isn't leaving.

The 'Hole Truth

You don't want her to stay at your place, but you wouldn't mind seeing her again. Clothed and unclothed. Tread lightly, because you don't want to piss her off enough to not have another shot at the Big Beef and Cheddar in her pants. No, I will never look at an Arby's sandwich the same way after that analogy either.

STEP 1 ▸ NEVER TAKE THE FUN INTO THE BEDROOM.

The bedroom means sleep. The bedroom means somewhere warm and comfy to lie down after you've bumped uglies. It also means she really doesn't have to get up again until morning. Keep the boning to the main areas of your place; the kitchen, the living room, or any available couch or open spot on the floor will do. Any place that, once the fucking is finito, it's really an uncomfortable place to be naked and sweaty. It will force her to get dressed again, and putting on clothes is one step away from walking out the front door.

STEP 2 ▸ GET UP AND GET BUSY.

Don't just lie around making cute talk. Get up and start doing things. Really dull and boring things. If it's a weekday, start getting ready for work the next day. Pack a lunch, pick out clothes, and show her you're getting back into real life. If it's a weekend, start getting ready for your plans the next day. "Oh, I totally forgot to pack my bags for that fishing trip I'm going on at 5 A.M. I guess I should start now."

STEP 3 ▸ STOP MESSING AROUND.

If you want her to leave, stop giving her reasons to stay. Don't mention something good coming on TV or how delightful you are at making late-night grub. Make it so boring that she will want to leave. Most important, don't keep having sex. Yes, I said stop screwing. Even an asshole knows when enough is enough. If you keep screwing around she will think she is crashing for the night, because only a douche bag would make a woman leave at 4 in the morning.

STEP 4 ▸ IF ALL ELSE FAILS, TAKE IT TO ANOTHER LOCATION.

She isn't getting the hint, so it looks like both of you will have to leave the premises. Ask her if she wants to go grab some food, or even go so far as offering to take her home. Just get out of your place.

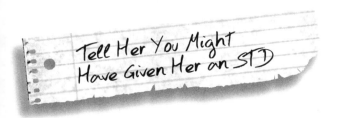

Tell Her You Might Have Given Her an STD

You've had your fun in the sack over the years and it
shows from the notches on your bedpost and the bumps
on your bologna. You finally got it checked out, and
while the dinky will live to doink another day, you do
have something that will involve ointments or pills to
control the spread.

The Problem

If you were single, or not in a sexual relationship at the
moment, you could probably just sit the bench for a little
while until you were 100 percent. Unfortunately, you're
steadily dunking the love muscle into her and she probably should get checked out as well. There is someone else
involved, and the doctor isn't going to break the news to
her. It's up to you.

The 'Hole Truth

Sitting a woman down to tell her you've given her something grody in her grass isn't an easy conversation. It's probably best to avoid it at all cost, but the topic might come up should she have a flare-up or find your bottle of pills in the medicine cabinet. You have several options regarding how you handle the situation.

OPTION 1 ▸ IT WAS THAT OTHER BITCH.

If you come right out and say you've got the ball bumps, her first thought is "Oh Mandingo this dude is dirtier than I thought," and the blame is all on your balls . . . shoulders . . . whichever. If you place the blame on the women in your past, then the first thought in her head is "Oh that chick was dirty, too bad she gave it to him too" and it makes you seem like just an unlucky casualty. This works great if she already hates your ex. Tell her she was in contact and told you about the issue, so you went to have it checked out.

OPTION 2 ▸ BLAME HER.

Tell her you've got something and it must have come from her because you've been especially careful for several years. You even wrapped it with girlfriends until they did a test to prove they were cleaner than a newborn's taint. It must be one of her man-whore ex-boyfriends that gave it to her and now you have it.

OPTION 3 ▸ IGNORE IT UNTIL IT GOES AWAY.

Let the meds do their job and wait for the infection to clear up. It's going to be hard to avoid sex, so you're going to have to start doing some creative fibbing. "I'd love to have sex tonight but I just got done boinking your sister." Good deflection. It doesn't matter anyway; now you've got to break it off with her because she's got it and you don't want it again. Also avoid the breakup sex. She is diseased, remember?

⊢ DON'T BE A DOUCHE ⊢

If you meet a chick before the infection is in deflection, wait it out before playin' the flip side. Only a douche would knowingly spread this shit around.

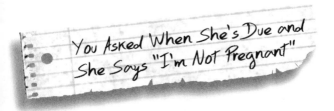

You Asked When She's Due and She Says "I'm Not Pregnant"

The problem with people is that they feel they must constantly make small talk with complete strangers. God forbid there is silence in a room, an elevator, or when you mistakenly walk into the ladies' dressing room at Victoria's Secret. Small talk only leads to odd exchanges and awkward slips of the tongue.

The Problem

A woman is chatting you up in line at the grocery store. You oblige because you've already read all the magazines on the stand and have nothing better to do while waiting for the woman writing a check at the front of the line. You don't want to tell her anything about yourself, so you notice she is sporting a little poonch and ask when she is going to have her baby. Her face changes expression (and color) as she informs you she isn't pregnant.

The 'Hole Truth

It's an honest mistake, because some women get fatter as the clothes for women get smaller, but she is obviously offended and you feel awful. With some quick thinking, you may be able to recover, but it will take a minor miracle and the greatest comeback ever.

OPTION 1 ▸ ASK HER IF SHE JUST HAD A BABY.

Your original question might only be a couple months late. It's hard for a woman to lose the weight after a baby, so she might just be lugging around the aftereffects of carrying around another human for nine months and then squirting the kid out a hole that wasn't meant to pass anything bigger than a summer sausage. Feel bad, don't you? Now call your mother.

OPTION 2 ▸ SUGGEST HEALTHIER FOOD OPTIONS.

Maybe she doesn't understand how food works. She is obviously ingesting too much high fructose corn syrup, and all of the fat is collecting around her midsection. Tell her it's probably a good idea to start shopping in an organic market and adding cardio into her daily routine to blast the fat. You might save her life as you're trying to save face. Of course, she might punch that same face for suggesting she is tubby, so this is a warning.

OPTION 3 ▸ ASK HER IF SHE WANTS TO GET PREGNANT.

It's worth a try. Even though you just called her fat in a roundabout sort of way. It might be the greatest pickup line ever, depending on her reaction. Is that mace on her key chain?

OPTION 4 ▸ PAY FOR HER GROCERIES.

You just asked her if she was pregnant (she isn't), told her how to eat (she didn't need the advice), asked if she'd been pregnant recently (again, not even close), and made advances to get her preggo so you can kind of be correct in your questioning. Buying her stuff is the least you could do for this poor woman. The second-best thing you can do is never make small talk again.

┤ DON'T BE A DOUCHE ├

Too late.

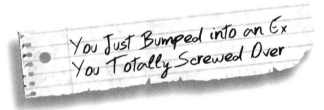

You Just Bumped into an Ex You Totally Screwed Over

It's a small world. Especially when you continue to frequent the same bars, restaurants, supermarkets, and office building as your ex-girlfriend. You know the girl; brown hair, great body, you dumped her via text message on the way to Vegas the same weekend as her sister's wedding. Yes, that girl. What do you mean "be more specific"?!?

The Problem

The girl is standing right in front of you for the first time since you dicked her over. You have no idea what is about to happen and you're torn between cupping your balls or faking a heart attack just to avoid the whole situation.

The 'Hole Truth

There was a reason you dumped her. You just can't remember exactly why, but the important thing is that you've got to prove that you're both better off not being together. She will/has found a better guy and you've got a lot less of her in your life. It was all for the better. She is going to want to get her revenge at this moment, though, so here is how to handle anything she may throw your way.

OPTION 1 ▸ IF SHE WANTS ANSWERS, GIVE HER THE TRUTH.

Women need something called "closure," which up until now we thought was some type of ointment for her vagina during the bloody days. It means that they need to know answers before they can move on. So give her answers. You broke up with her because she was too needy, clingy, smelly, crazy, or whatever the reason was that you dumped her and moved on with your life. You're just helping her out for the next guy. If she tones down the shit she does, she is less likely to scare another dude off.

OPTION 2 ▸ IF SHE WANTS TO CRY, TELL HER TO TOUGHEN UP.

She might get all emotional and cry about the way you left her hanging. You don't have time to sit around and listen to her babble like she did when you were dating. Especially because at least then there was a chance at sex. Tell her she has to move on and it's probably best that you did bump into one another so you can tell her to her face that it's time to stop crying about the past and get on with her life.

OPTION 3 ▸ IF SHE GETS VIOLENT, YOU GET DEFENSELESS.

If you've got a fighter on your hands, you've got to be ready from the outset. You know already if she is the type of bitch that is going to hit a guy (probably because she has done it in the past), so keep your eyes on her hands at all times and get ready to take a couple shots. The two most important things to remember are a) never fight back and b) make a big enough scene so that people see you're being attacked and it will make it easier when Five-O arrive.

DON'T BE A DOUCHE

Don't apologize or blame yourself for the breakup. You did nothing wrong. Even if you did, you shouldn't think you did. And only a douche would apologize when he knows he made the right choice.

You Sexted the Wrong Person

Sexting can be hot in the hands of an expert. You already know you're an expert, because every asshole should be good at wordplay, but finding a woman who's good at texting perverted ideas and NSFW pictures brings the naughty to a whole new level.

The Problem

You were feeling a little chubby under the zipper and decided to sext your favorite target. You said some pretty nasty things and maybe even sent a little picture to get her juices flowing. Unfortunately, you're terrible with your phone and you sent it to the wrong person.

The 'Hole Truth

It's out there and there is no going back. It's time to do some damage control. The amount of damage depends on the recipient of your sex slang and picture message of your egg-white cannon.

IF IT'S ANOTHER GIRL . . .

Wait to see if or how she responds. It might not be so bad. If she's into it, she might sext back and now you've got two possible digital humping partners. If she texts back that you're a pervert, still don't say anything back. Just delete her phone number and block her from calling or texting.

IF IT'S AN EX . . .

Let's hope you are on friendly terms. If she dated you long enough she knows you're a sexual deviant, isn't surprised by your actions, and it's possibly the reason you two split up in the first place. Who knows, it could lead to one last pump in the dumper. Of course, she might be a stuck-up bitch about it. Another reason you split up.

IF IT'S A COWORKER . . .

Damage control! Shut your phone off. Go to the store and buy a brand-new cell phone. Get into the office as early as possible the next day. Write an e-mail and send it to everyone at work explaining your cell phone was stolen and you had to buy a new one. You lost all of your info so request everyone to send their cell phone numbers to put into the new phone. The coworker might share the sexting story. You've got to act APPALLED. You've got to say you hope the pervert that stole your phone didn't do that to anyone else. "Oh god, Mee Maw's phone number is in that phone! Oh, Mee Maw!" Then run away.

IF IT'S A DUDE . . .
Leave the country. You'll be missed.

| DON'T BE A DOUCHE |

Too late. You sexted the wrong person. You became a douche the moment you hit Send.

Get Her To Have Sex On Camera

Sex sometimes gets a little vanilla, so an asshole has to spice things up a little bit. Toys get old and she never lets you bring anyone else into the bedroom. It's time to take it to the voyeur level. Asshole and his lady make a porno.

The Problem

She barely gets undressed with the lights on. Convincing her to bare it all and do the dirty in front of a flip cam isn't going to be an easy sell. You've got to make it an enjoyable experience and convince her you are actually doing this for the both of you. Trick her. That is a nice way of saying you've got to trick her.

The 'Hole Truth

Many women are more into voyeurism than they will admit. It actually could be because they don't know they are into it yet. It's up to you to show them how exciting and sexually exhilarating a camera can be while you're deep in the throes of sextacy. Lights, camera, get nude!

STEP 1 ▸ SHOW HER HOW CELEBS DO IT.

Kim Kardashian. Paris Hilton. Screech from *Saved by the Bell*. Many famous celebs have bared all in front of the camera and actually came out on the other end even more popular. It's not saying she is going to get her own reality show out of this deal, but it proves that even famous people with much more to lose have done the dirty in front of a flip cam.

STEP 2 ▸ SHOW HER ALL THE TERRIBLY UNATTRACTIVE PEOPLE WHO DO IT.

Take her on an online tour of all the ugly people posing naked for the entire world. It's kind of disturbing the number of ugly people having sex on cam and slapping it on the Internet. If they can show off their flab and small donkey kongs to millions of strangers she can at least get naked for a video to be enjoyed as a couple. On a side note, ugly people, please stop posing and putting it online. That is all.

STEP 3 ▸ START SMALL—WITH PICTURES.

Fine, so she won't go all Jenna Jameson the first time around. Baby steps, asshole. Get her to pose for a few naughty pictures. It will loosen her up and might even get her excited for the video idea. Show her the pics and tell her how great she looks. Airbrush if necessary.

STEP 4 ▸ ASSURE HER IT'S FOR YOUR EYES ONLY.

Part of her trepidation is the fear that should things go wrong in the relationship, her naked ass will end up all over the Internet, on T-shirts, and sold to the Girls Gone Wild franchise. Assure her that no one will ever see these photos or vids and promise her you won't even mention it to friends. Seriously, erase all of it. Even your screen-saver. Wait, e-mail over that pic first. Okay, now delete it.

⊣ DON'T BE A DOUCHE ⊢

Don't just grab a camera one night and start filming. It will turn her off to the idea immediately because she hasn't even had a chance to think about it. Don't ever do it without her consent. It's pretty illegal.

You're Caught Masturbating, Now What?

You could never love someone as much as you love your-self. Wait. I meant to say masturbate, not love. It's a plea-surable experience that you may get the urge to do at odd times. Times when it's easier to get caught. How did you know the custodian was cleaning the office early today? At least you were nice enough to aim for the mop bucket.

The Problem

The urge took over and you needed a quick release. Unfortunately you didn't do your due diligence and got caught white-handed. You were flopping beef and got caught. It's not the end of the world, but it's a pretty awkward situation.

The 'Hole Truth

Everyone masturbates. Everyone has masturbated in an odd situation or setting. You can recover from this calamity, but it will take some quick thinking from the head on your shoulders and not the head in your Dockers.

STEP 1 ▸ FINISH UP.

The last thing you want is a set of blue balls. If the sex cannon still has a round in the chamber, it's in your best interest to fire it off. Unless you've lost your chubby; then cut your losses, pull your pants up, and face the situation like a man. How do you still have wood? You're a perv.

STEP 2 ▸ COLLECT YOUR THOUGHTS AND YOUR PARAPHERNALIA.

The worst thing to do is to get all flustered and try to explain mid-yank. The person isn't sticking around to hear your rebuttal. It's certainly not going to make any sense in the moment. You'll say something stupid like "it's not what you think," but unless the person is a moron and thinks you're sailboat racing, it's exactly what they think. Gather your defense in your head while you gather up your tools of the trade. And honestly, could you have chosen a bigger bottle of Jergens lotion? You expecting a long winter?

STEP 3 ▸ REMEMBER THAT THE PERSON WHO CAUGHT YOU IS JUST AS EMBARRASSED.

Imagine walking in on a guy. Aside from laughing your ass off, you'd probably be embarrassed for yourself and for the poor bastard caught white-handed. The person who caught you is feeling just as odd about the situation at hand (PUN!). He or she will probably want to pretend it never happened. You should follow that lead.

STEP 4 ▸ NEVER TALK TO THAT PERSON AGAIN.

Should be simple—no one wants to pal around with a public masturbator—but make sure you never have contact with the person again. If it's a coworker, quit your job. If it's a family member, disown her and move to another state. If it's a roommate, move out, but not before catching him in the act first. Fair is fair.

┤ DON'T BE A DOUCHE ├

If you're bringing your one-man pants circus on the road, try not to stain anything. That's just disgusting.

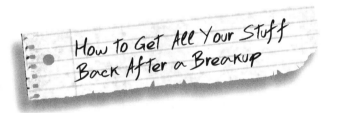

How to Get All Your Stuff Back After a Breakup

It wasn't a pleasant breakup and there is a good chance you'll never see her again. You're cool with that because it makes it all that much easier. Clean break. No reason to prolong the experience. Now that you've got more free time, might be a good chance to hang out with some friends out of town. Give them a call. Where the hell is your cell phone anyway? Oh, turdballs.

The Problem

You've got stuff all over her apartment that you want back. She isn't really happy with you right now and could be lighting a bonfire of treasures in your name as I speak. You've got to get all your stuff back in one piece, not a million little pieces.

The 'Hole Truth

It's your personal property, so destroying it is actually against the law. Still, it's going to be hard to call the cops to explain that she took a butcher knife to your lucky Royals hat (yes, that's an oxymoron), so you really have to move quickly to get all your possessions back before she does something crazy.

STEP 1 ▸ TAKE A PERSONAL INVENTORY.

Try and remember everything you've left over at her place, everything you've left in her car and anything you might have lent her so that you know exactly what is missing. Make an actual list so that you remember because you're only going to be able to ask for your stuff back once.

STEP 2 ▸ MAKE IT SEEM UNIMPORTANT.

The last thing you want to do is act like the stuff is important, because if she is vindictive she will make sure to never give it to you or just destroy it with a rented jackhammer. Call her up to "see how she is," and in the course of the conversation casually mention one item in particular that you're looking to retrieve. It's all jammed in one box already anyway, but you'll figure that out when it gets thrown at your head.

STEP 3 ▸ SHOW UP WITH HER STUFF.

It's only fair to have all her stuff ready for an even exchange. Make sure you have everything so that there is no reason to meet up again for an exchange of unpleasantries and goods. Check every inch of your place for all her junk and give it back to her. Even her copy of *Sex and the City 2*. You're just going to have to buy your own.

STEP 4 ▸ IF IT WAS A GIFT, IT REMAINS A GIFT.

You can't take back anything that isn't really yours, and this includes gifts to her and even things that were once yours but you no longer have possession of, like a favorite shirt or lucky hat. Oh and the engagement ring. Sorry bro, it's gone forever. She is gonna sell it and spend the money to forget you. Think of it as buying your freedom.

┤ DON'T BE A DOUCHE ├

Don't use the spare key to her place to take all your stuff when she isn't home. It's almost like breaking and entering and it's a wuss move. Unless, of course, she is bat-shit crazy and likely to shank you the next time you're face-to-face. In that case, break into that joint Snake Eyes–style and get your stuff.

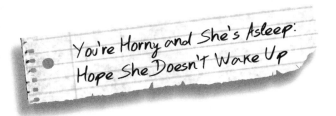

You're Horny and She's Asleep: Hope She Doesn't Wake Up

Sex is great, but there comes a point in a relationship when the planets are off kilter and the cosmos is all loopy and you and your partner are just on different sexual schedules. She is horny and you're exhausted or you're horny and she is in the middle of holy week. It's getting to the point where you have to sync up schedules on your smart phones and set up reminders to do the horizontal tummy bump.

The Problem

It's late. You're flipping around on the tube and come across a skin flick on regular cable. It's got you poking up the bed sheets with your nutty buddy. You are horny. She is fast asleep. For now.

The 'Hole Truth

She might not wake up and want sex, but if you play the situation correctly you could be dropping your change in the night depository before Letterman is over.

STEP 1 ▸ PULL THE COVERS OFF OF HER.

She will wake up immediately, and probably bitch you out for taking the covers, but at least she is awake now. Apologize and cuddle up next to her and tell her you'll keep her warm. She will know exactly what you're up to, but that doesn't matter because frankly she always knows what you're up to. You're terrible at hiding the truth.

STEP 2 ▸ FAKE A BURGLARY.

Did you hear that? It was coming from downstairs. I'll check it out. Wait here and have the phone next to you in case of emergency. (Wait five minutes.) It was nothing. You scared? Don't be scared. I'm here to protect you. Come here, I'll hold you. Squeeze you tight. Touch your boobs.

STEP 3 ▸ RECALL THE PAST.

Wake her up and tell her you were thinking back to the first time you kissed or the moment you fell in love with her. Make sure you get the info correct or you'll spend the whole night being called a dick for not remembering the little things. Does it still feel like the first time, every time we kiss? Chicks dig that shit. It's like their very own Lifetime movie without the lady from *Designing Women*. No, the fat one that was married to Major Dad.

STEP 4 ▸ TAP HER ON THE SHOULDER AND TELL HER YOU ARE HORNY AND WANT TO HAVE SEX.

Honesty is usually the best policy, and an asshole always asks for what he wants.

⊢ DON'T BE A DOUCHE ⊢

Enough with the boner rub against her backside. That is an automatic no, and pounding your pud in the bathroom is no way to go through life. Unless you're in prison.

A**holeology: The Cheat Sheet

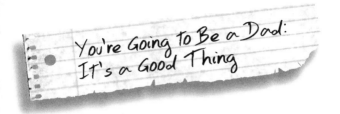

You're Going To Be a Dad:
It's a Good Thing

After countless piss tests and an actual medical examination it's been brought to your attention that you're going to be a father. You okay? Drink some water, sit down for a second. Relax, it's an incredibly joyous occasion. You're going to have a little asshole. A baby who can learn the ways of the asshole from you at an early age so he can avoid all the missteps and mistakes you made during your formative years.

The Problem

Exactly how do you raise a baby asshole? There isn't much information in the field (only because we've yet to write the book on it), so you're going to have to take all you've learned as an adult and modify it to work in the world of diapers, day care, and *Yo Gabba Gabba*.

The 'Hole Truth

This could be the most important project of your life. If you're successful, an asshole spawn will carry on your name and legacy. If you fail, it could be the start of a little douche bag that will ruin your life. Hey, no pressure, right?

STEP 1 ▸ DON'T TELL THE MOM YOUR PLANS.

Chances are the kid's mother isn't going to be too receptive to you having this type of influence on her child at such an important age in his development. It won't be easy for her handling two different assholes, especially when the bigger asshole is supposed to be helping with more important things, like feeding and changing. Keep the whole idea under your hat. The same place where your hair used to be.

STEP 2 ▸ TEACH HIM EARLY AND OFTEN.

There have been studies that show the child is actually capable of hearing and learning while in the womb. That's why you'll sometimes see a woman with an iPod strapped to her stomach and headphones around her giant belly. If possible, try to swap out her Celine Dion collection with the audio version of this or the original *A**holeology* book, or even record your own lessons in MP3 form. If it isn't possible to corrupt him in the womb, begin the moment he is born, talking to him every second he is awake. Optimal times are during feedings, when he is most attentive. Unless she breastfeeds. You can't all fit on the same rocking chair.

STEP 3 ▸ WRITE IT ALL DOWN FOR HIM.

After each lesson, jot down the most important points for him and put them together into a handy eBook or PDF file. When he gets old enough and asks you to tell him a bedtime story, you'll have a nice little piece of literature to read as he nods off to sleep. "Lie down son, and listen how you'll eventually have people eating from your hands. Once upon a time there was a little asshole . . ."

STEP 4 ▸ CHART HIS PROGRESS TO HELP TRAIN OTHER FUTURE ASSHOLES.

As he makes strides into a little asshole that dad could be proud of, be sure to jot down his progress and mistakes for future study. Keep your notes in a handy binder and share them with other asshole dads. Who knows, you might end up getting a book deal out of it. That is, if I don't write it first.

⊢ DON'T BE A DOUCHE ⊣

Don't be too hard on him if he doesn't take to it all quickly. Think how long it took you to become the asshole you are now.

Chapter 5.
The Daily Grind

How to Handle the Annoying Movie Patron

People have forgotten how to act in a movie theater. It's almost like they forget there are about 200 people sitting around them trying to pay attention to a movie. People talk to each other, talk on a cell, put their feet all over the seats, and act as if they are the most important people in the room. This just in: they are not, you are, and you know how to act in a movie theater. You're gladly going to show them how it's done.

The Problem

The guy in the seat in front of you will not shut the fuck up. He started yapping during previews and hasn't shut up since. It's ruining the movie for everyone around him. Don't be a douche and run to get the manager, because there is nothing he can really do in this situation except offer you free tickets to another show, where you'll have to deal with a whole new set of dick-faces.

The 'Hole Truth

No one else is going to say anything because they don't have the balls. Luckily there is an asshole in the house. You've got to teach this douche some manners.

ACT 1 ▶ SILENCE IS GOLDEN.

Visit the men's room with an empty water bottle or soda cup (which you emptied by chugging the contents as fast as possible about ten minutes earlier). Fill the container to the brim with some toasty-warm piss. Go back to your seat and set the bottle in front of your feet. OOPS! Look at that—it spilled all in front of you and onto his shoes and socks. Isn't that a shame.

INTERMISSION ▸ MAKE EVERY ATTEMPT TO LEARN HIS FIRST AND LAST NAME.

Ask him if you have to. Say he looks familiar and ask him if he ever worked at some company or lived in some building. Once you get his name, go to the lobby and call the theater and ask to have him paged and tell the theater manager it's a major medical emergency.

ACT 2 ▸ FUNNY AND GUMMY.

Ever gotten candy stuck to the bottom of your shoe in a movie theater? It's impossible to get it off, right? Now imagine it's stuck to the back of your shirt, coat, or even your hair. It would be near impossible to get out. Mr. Owl! How many licks does it take to get a Tootsie Pop to stick to a douche bag's leather coat? Let's find out . . .

THE FINAL SCENE ▸ USE YOUR PHONE TO LOOK UP SPOILERS FOR THE MOVIE.

Just before the most important scene, lean forward and whisper the ending in his ear. Then tell him he's got a bunch of candy stuck to the back of his jacket, and leave the theater. On the way out, complain to the manager and get comp tickets to another show.

┤ DON'T BE A DOUCHE ├

Don't. talk. during. movies.

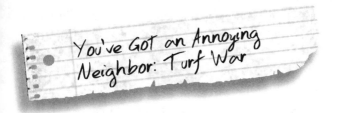

You've Got an Annoying Neighbor: Turf War

Love thy neighbor. Unless he is a major douche rocket. Then it's acceptable to hate him and fail to acknowledge his mere existence even when you are outside at the same time. He does have a nicer lawn, which is just more proof he doesn't really have a life.

The Problem

You love where you live, but your neighbor makes life hell. He does at least one thing per day that pisses you off while bringing down the property value. That glass ball on the pedestal in front of his house? Yeah, I have no goddamn clue what it is either, but it's just as big a waste of space as its owner. You aren't moving, so something has to be done.

The 'Hole Truth

It's your neighborhood too, and there is a good chance if he is pissing you off then he also has rubbed some of the other people in the 'hood the wrong way. The annoying neighbor can be controlled, but it will take some careful strategy and undercover operations.

STEP 1 ▸ GET THE PITCHFORKS.

You've got to have the rest of the neighborhood on your side. Figure out who has just as big a problem with good ol' Mr. Worthless and get them to join your side. Rally the troops and spread lies so everyone in the neighborhood hates the jerkoff. Even get the mailman involved.

STEP 2 ▸ SEND AN ANONYMOUS LETTER.

Nothing wrong with a scathing letter explaining all the reasons he is hated in the 'hood minus a signature at the bottom. Make sure to type it out so he can't figure out the handwriting by stealing mail and comparing, and drop it in his mailbox during the few moments he isn't staring out the window.

STEP 3 ▸ GET THE COPS INVOLVED.

Call the authorities any time you feel like watching a squad car hang in front of his house with the lights on for about a half hour. Make up stories like you heard screams coming from his house and you walked by in the afternoon and smelled an odd odor coming from the shed behind his house. Walk by as the police are questioning him and ask "What's going on, officer?" Try calling the local news too. They might show up on a slow day.

STEP 4 ▸ WRITE ON HIS LAWN WITH WEED KILLER.

It will probably take at least a couple seasons to get the grass to grow back, but until then, the entire neighborhood will know your neighbor is an "ass cannon" or whatever else you'd like to call him. Make sure to check out your work using Google Earth.

STEP 5 ▸ MARK HIS HOUSE AS A SEX OFFENDER'S.

Unless it already is. Then just move.

─┤ **DON'T BE A DOUCHE** ├─

Watch your language. There are kids in the neighborhood.

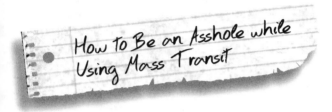

How to Be an Asshole while Using Mass Transit

So selling your friend's car and getting your own back wasn't the most brilliant idea. Wasn't even legal. Even assholes have bad ideas once in a while. Just remember Demandment IX: *The asshole learns from his (few) mistakes.* This time you learned not to piss off your friend because as payback he took *your* car and dumped it over the side of a ravine.

The Problem
You've now joined one of the masses and are taking public transportation. Just until the garage pulls your car out and repairs it (note to self: it's gonna be pricey; better sell another friend's car). Taking public buses and trains sucks the soul right out of a person. You've got to stake your claim to make it as painless as possible.

The 'Hole Truth
It's time to turn to the Demandments and remember that the asshole cares about the asshole the most. Your comfort, safety, and blood pressure should all be front of

mind. Here's how to make your journey with the common folk less hellish.

STEP 1 ▸ KEEP THE SEAT NEXT TO YOU EMPTY.

You will have a much better ride if there isn't someone sitting right next to you, rubbing elbows like a horny tween on a movie date. Put a bag, jacket, or wad of gum on the extra seat so no one will sit down. If it gets crowded and someone asks you to move your belongings, tell him you're saving the seat for the son of Lucifer and he'll be arriving by fire at any moment. The person will think you're crazy and go elsewhere.

STEP 2 ▸ REQUEST THE WINDOW.

If you want to sit next to the window, you should get your wish. If someone is sitting there you should ask him to move. Invent some medical condition that requires you to sit near an open area at all times or your sinuses will act up and you'll blow snot rockets all over the place.

STEP 3 ▸ STAND YOUR GROUND.

If you are forced to stand for the entire ride, don't let people bump and smash against you at every turn. Set a barrier around yourself using outstretched hands and strategically placed kicks to the shins if others invade your personal space.

STEP 4 ▸ AVOID PEOPLE.

It's a good rule when riding public transit—and just in general—to avoid talking, engaging, or even briefly acknowledging anyone because nothing good will come of it. It's not like you're going to stumble into some superstar in the making, or anyone important, while sweating your ass off riding the NYC subway on a Tuesday morning. Don't talk. Don't look. Just keep your head down and pray your car is saved soon.

| **DON'T BE A DOUCHE** |

If you stink, don't ride. No one wants to smell you.

Dealing with Customer Service

You've been screwed over one too many times by one too many companies. They give you the runaround, leave you on hold for hours, and get you so frustrated you'd rather just live with the fraudulent charges on your credit card or terrible cable service than have to deal with another phone call explaining your issue.

The Problem
For the most part, every company has terrible customer service. They don't really care, either. For every customer they lose, another is jumping onboard, so why should they care when they're still making money?

The 'Hole Truth
There is a way to turn the tables on customer service people and the huge, heartless companies they collect a check from every other week.

STEP 1 ▸ "NO" IS NOT AN OPTION.

Never let a customer service rep tell you that it isn't possible to accomplish what you're requesting. Tell him matter-of-factly you're not leaving or hanging up until you get results. If he does tell you no, hang up or leave and try again another time. Most companies don't spend the time to perfectly train every single person who walks through the revolving door of customer service. Keep calling until you find someone unfamiliar with protocol and willing to do whatever you ask to get you off the phone.

STEP 2 ▸ CLIMB THE LADDER.

The last thing any working grunt wants to deal with on a given day is crap from his boss. This is why an ass-hole always asks to speak to the next person in command. If a customer service rep is giving you lip, ask to speak to the manager. If the manager is a wall of moron, ask to speak to his or her supervisor. Keep climbing up the ladder until your issue is resolved. Make a nuisance of yourself by calling every single person in the chain every day of the week until someone solves your problem.

STEP 3 ▸ TAKE YOUR PROBLEM TO THE MASSES.

Word of mouth in online social media circles is having a huge effect on the average consumer, and businesses have noticed this trend. Businesses are terrified of word leaking about just how terrible they are at helping the customer. Use social media sites like Facebook and Twitter to turn one little voice into a thousand negative voices. There might even already be a "Wal-Mart Sucks" Facebook group, or an entire anti-McDonald's website appropriately named McSucks. If the group doesn't exist, get one started and bother people to join.

STEP 4 ▸ CANCEL YOUR ACCOUNT.

An asshole never lets someone else come out on top. Many people think the customer service rep, or the company in general, is in control. As the consumer, you hold the power in every situation. If they're smart, they'll do everything they can to keep your business.

⊣ DON'T BE A DOUCHE ⊢

Bitching out the little guy might feel good, but puts you in douche territory—every asshole knows that guy's only making minimum wage and can't really help you out.

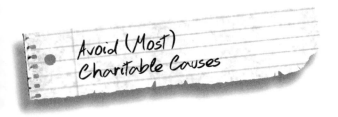

Avoid (Most) Charitable Causes

Even an asshole should donate money to a worthy cause. Herein lies the rub: there are too many worthy causes. You are aware of this because at least once a day someone is hitting you up to donate to something or other.

The Problem

It seems like every time you turn around, someone else is begging you for money in the name of charity. Selling cookies for a kid in the Girl Scouts, collecting a dollar for autism, or donating aluminum can tops to save some kid on life support—did that really work? One million can tops!

You get five more minutes to live, Johnny! Yippee!!—nearly everyone is looking for some type of handout.

The 'Hole Truth

It's not that you don't want to be a charitable asshole, but giving to so many causes will send you to the poorhouse. Then maybe someone can take a collection for your own broke ass. How does an asshole choose just a select few, and how does he make people aware he is giving, but not to every organization in need? Here are some options.

OPTION 1 ▸ MAKE A BIG DEAL OUT OF IT.

Now is the time to brag about your charity. Spread it around like your sperm at summer camp. Post it to your Facebook, Twitter, MySpace, and JDate profile. Let everyone know you gave money to charity X and they should give money too. This should keep anyone else from asking you for money because they know you just gave a large amount to another cause. Possible downside is more people could ask you for a handout because they didn't realize you were such a charitable asshole. Luckily you can use the "I just gave to another charity" as a Get Out of Giving Shit Free card.

OPTION 2 ▸ OFFER YOUR MINUTES, NOT YOUR MOOLA.

The next time a person is hitting you up for a financial donation, offer your time instead. If it is indeed a charity in need, it will take any help, whether monetary or just a helping hand. Tell the middleman you'd love to get involved; if he just points you to the nearest location, you'll lend a hand doing whatever they need: build a house, stuff goody bags, or figure out a more cost-effective way to launder money through the charity.

OPTION 3 ▸ FIND YOUR OWN DAMN CHARITY.

The begging won't end and it's getting uncomfortable. Stump for your own cause. Find a charity and start collecting money. Hit up all the same people who bother you for donations. Make it awkward.

⊣ **DON'T BE A DOUCHE** ⊢

You've got to give something to charity. Only a douche doesn't donate at least a little money to a worthy cause. Hell, even if you don't have time or money, donate blood. You could save a life. (That was probably the most serious thing you'll read in this book. I feel odd. Someone make a pussy joke.)

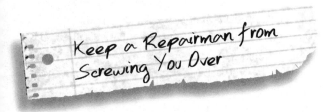

Keep a Repairman from Screwing You Over

An asshole is busy. He usually handles things around the home, especially small improvement projects. Occasionally, life gets out of control and an asshole can't tackle all the projects. That is when he calls in an expert.

The Problem

Repairmen aren't the most honest gaggle of blue-collar folk. Shocking. It's hard to find an honest day's work for anything less than triple the markup for labor.

The 'Hole Truth

There are honest workers out there; you've just got to do your homework and refuse to get screwed. Follow these steps to get exactly what you pay for from a handyman. Yes, I also think Handyman is a funny gay porn name. Just not as funny as you do.

STEP 1 ▸ GET SOME NAMES FROM PEOPLE.

Think of any friends or family that just bored the hell out of you with home improvement stories. It's always best to ask people who have already had success with a repairman. If they find someone who does fantastic work and is trustworthy, they will be happy to pass the information along to friends. If it gets the repairman another job, it could get them a discount next time he does work on their house. It there's a house you admire, ask who did the work. Also ask for prices. You'll need that info when it comes to negotiating your project.

STEP 2 ▸ GOOGLE HIS ASS.

Behold the Internet! Keeper of free porn, videos of crotch shots aplenty, and chronicler of all the times someone fucked someone else over. If this guy has screwed someone over, there is a solid chance the entire ordeal is there for the reading on the Net. People love to complain, and if there isn't anyone to listen they will take it to the anonymous world of the web. It may take some digging, but it could save you money and aggravation.

STEP 3 ▸ GET SOME REFERENCES.

He seems legit and his price is affordable. Every job asks for references before hiring a potential employee, so why can't you ask for references before hiring a stranger to work in your house? Since he is so confident about his work and pricing, ask him for the names and numbers of people he has worked for in the past few months.

STEP 4 ▸ ASK FOR A WRITTEN ESTIMATE.

This is so important, I'm willing to waste a little more ink on it and put it all in capital letters. MAKE HIM PUT EVERYTHING IN WRITING. Ask how much it will cost, what he will do, how much the materials will be, and when he plans on finishing. Ask him to slap it all on company letterhead and have him sign it. If he refuses, or just doesn't know how to type and print, do it for him. Print it out and tell him to sign it. If he doesn't agree, no deal.

┤ DON'T BE A DOUCHE ├

Never pay in full before the job is done. What incentive is there for him to do a good job, or hell, even come back after he has all his money? If he asks to be paid in full before the job is done, he is looking to screw you over. He is a douche bag for doing it, but you're a bigger douche for falling for it.

Make Shopping as Painless as Possible

An asshole always has to look sharp. You should have learned that in the first book. Looking good takes time. It also can be a painful process that includes dealing with the hassle of shopping malls and men's clothing stores.

The Problem

Shopping is usually a terrible experience because it involves too many other people. Malls suck. Men's clothing stores are full of overbearing salespeople. If only you were loaded enough to shut down stores and shop alone like you're a celebrity. Start working on that, asshole. We'll teach you how to handle shopping until that happens.

The 'Hole Truth

Shopping will be a hundred times easier if you stick to simple rules to maximize efficiency and minimize the time you've got to spend wandering around a store listening to loud-ass Lady Gaga and nosey salespeople who can't understand what the hell "just looking" means.

RULE 1 ▸ MAKE A DAMN LIST.

Never go shopping thinking you need new shorts, or undecided about buying a new pair of jeans. Take a minute to do inventory of your clothes and write down all the clothes you'll need to pick up on this shopping trip. Hit everything on the list and mark it off when completed. This will make the trip quick and save the follow-up trip to the mall because you forgot you don't own an actual pair of shoes.

RULE 2 ▸ WHAT'S CHEAP IS EXPENSIVE.

Clothes are the only place you shouldn't attempt to save a couple bucks. There is a reason stores like Old Navy, American Eagle, and places of the like can charge a little less for clothing; it's all poorly made. After a couple washings, the clothes break down faster than a prisoner at Abu Ghraib. Spend a little more money on expensive clothes and shoes and they will last at least a few years—so long as they're still in style.

RULE 3 ▸ LOOK INTO THE PERSONAL SHOPPER OPTION.

A hidden secret of many chain and high-end clothing stores is the personal shopper option. Stores will offer a personal shopper free of charge to discuss your shopping goals, put together outfits for you based on your personal preferences, and have them ready for you to try on before you even get to the store. There is no pressure to buy, and it takes most of the thinking out of shopping. Another option is just buying the exact outfit displayed on the store mannequins. Effective, but not as much fun as having a shopping slave.

┤ DON'T BE A DOUCHE ├

If you're out of college, older than twenty-one, and don't have lacrosse practice, you shouldn't shop at Hollister, Abercrombie, or any other trendy kiddie stores. Only a douche dresses younger than it says on his driver's license.

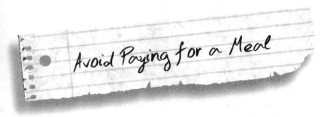

Avoid Paying for a Meal

People forget things all the time, like where they put their keys or the name of their current spouse. It's the drawback of living in a society driven by constant information overload. For all the shit you take in, some things just have to fall out. Blame your pea brain.

The Problem

You're out to eat. You reach for your wallet and realize it's just where you last saw it—on the dresser in your bedroom. You've got no cash and no plastic and the main course is on its way out of the kitchen. You can't pay for this meal. Correction. You're not gonna pay for this meal.

The 'Hole Truth

The last thing a restaurant wants is a problem. The very last thing it wants is a scene. You've got to create both, so eventually the manager will have no choice but to comp you a meal and get you the hell out of the joint. Here are some options on how to get the meal on the house.

OPTION 1 ▸ COMPLAIN.

Early, often, and loudly. I already said the very last thing a restaurant wants is a scene; the very, very last thing it wants is you involving the other customers. Complain loud enough for the tables next to you to overhear. Bring them into the situation. "This isn't what I ordered off the menu. Hey buddy, ever seen a surf and turf this lackluster? Take a good look." The manager will want to quash the complaint and keep you happy and quiet.

OPTION 2 ▸ THERE IS SOMETHING IN YOUR FOOD BECAUSE YOU PUT IT THERE.

It doesn't matter what it is; just that it's disgusting and inedible. The more disgusting the better. Run into the men's room and grab a urinal cake to sink to the bottom of your New England clam chowder. Grab a pen off the bar and drop it into your Shrimp Fra Diavolo. How did it get in there? How the fuck should you know how it got in there! Why don't you go ask the chef if he is missing a pen, or check the men's room for a not-so-fresh smelling urinal? You're not paying for this meal, nor will they allow you to pay.

OPTION 3 ▸ CHOKE.

Take a big old hunk of steak. Put it in the back of your mouth. Stand up with your hands wrapped around your neck and start gagging like hell. Wait for a Good Samaritan to come running over to your table to save the day, and then spit that hunk of cow ass as far across the room as possible. Break down and cry to hit a real home run. Oh, it's on the house? Well, I think I might be able to swallow down a dessert.

> ### ┤ DON'T BE A DOUCHE ├
>
> Never dine and dash. You're not screwing over the restaurant, just the poor server, and all because you couldn't remember your wallet.

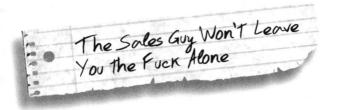

There is this odd approach in sales wherein people believe the more they pester to "help" you, the more you'll need their assistance and the more money they will make off of you. This usually happens when commission is involved. The easy way to tell if commission is involved in sales is that the sales guy is following you around the furniture store, car lot, or clothing store like a bored puppy looking to get his ass rubbed. "Can I help you? How about now? Now? Now?"

The Problem

You just want to look around without someone looking over your shoulder or jumping up from behind displays trying to help or answer any questions you don't even have yet because you haven't been able to concentrate on anything except the sales guy and his constant chatter.

The 'Hole Truth

The asshole customer is always right, and in this case, you are right to ask the sales guy to back off until you're ready to talk. Here are some ideas to get him off your back until you're ready to wheel and deal.

STEP 1 ▸ TELL HIM YOU'LL FIND HIM.

This is especially helpful for the guys who bum-rush you the minute you walk into the front door of the store. You can feel him approaching and immediately smell the stink of a morning's worth of coffee and his Drakkar-stained suit. Get his name, maybe even his business card, and tell him you just want to look around and when you are ready to talk you'll come find him. This will calm his fears of you grabbing any sales slug that happens to be close when you have a question.

STEP 2 ▸ BRING A DECOY.

You're looking for a couch or a new car and your friend is just looking for something to do on a Saturday morning. Bring him along to run decoy while you shop. Have him play it up like he is looking to buy and make him ask a ton of questions of the sales fella. Tell your friend to take the guy on a walk around the joint. You can use this time to look around without a hassle.

STEP 3 ▸ SET A BUDGET, EVEN IF THERE REALLY IS NONE.

You've narrowed it down to a few choices and you're ready to talk price and options. Tell the guy straight out you're only looking to spend X amount of dollars and you're not going over that price. This will keep him from showing you other, much more expensive, options and will cut the amount of time spent on the purchase.

STEP 4 ▸ LET'S MAKE A DEAL.

No price is ever set in stone. If he wants the sale bad enough, he will get you a better price. He will step away to talk to a manager, or crunch some numbers, or jack-knife another cup of coffee down his gullet and make it appear he is trying to get you a better deal. Whatever he has to do to make the price go down, let him do it. He will come back with an offer. If you like it, shake his hand and make it happen. If you don't, ALWAYS be prepared to walk away.

DON'T BE A DOUCHE

Don't let him sell you on upgrades, warranties, and incidentals in case there is a zombie attack and blood gets on your new couch. These are all just ways to jack up the price.

A**holeology: The Cheat Sheet

Chapter 6.
Fun and Leisure

The Cops Have Arrived, Now What?

The party was just getting started. The music was pumping, the booze was flowing, and everyone in the place was a bad decision away from an incredibly awesome evening. Who would knock on the door when the party was obviously still raging? Oh. Those guys.

The Problem

There are two uniformed officers in your doorway and they're not the strippers you ordered for later in the evening. If they are, you want your money back.

The 'Hole Truth

It's not a high-school kegger, so you're not in any trouble. Yet. If you make it hard on the boys in blue, they will make it hard on you, so tread lightly and you'll spend the evening in your own bed and not a cot down at county.

STEP 1 ▶ TALK OUTSIDE THE HOUSE.

The last thing you need is some moron stumbling by with a handheld mirror topped with the bouncing powder or the cops getting a peek at anything else illegal going on. Walk outside and shut the door behind you. The fresh air will help you clear your mind and get your thoughts together in order to answer their questions, or it might get you totally bombed. Why the night air increases your drunkenness I've got no idea, but I'm ready to pay NASA to get to the bottom of that issue, stat.

STEP 2 ▸ "YES" AND "NO" WILL BE GOOD ENOUGH.

Don't get chatty. Don't engage in long conversations or explanations about the evening's events. Yes, you realize it's late and no, you didn't realize the party had gotten so loud. Yes, you'll keep it down and no, they won't have to come back to speak with you again.

STEP 3 ▸ NAME-DROPPING WOULDN'T HURT.

Name anyone you might know in the department, from the chief down to the dispatcher who was in AA with you a few years back. Drop as many names as possible that might get you out of trouble without even a warning. Even though this isn't a moving vehicle (though your head is spinning like it's a flying saucer), if you've got a PBA card in your wallet this wouldn't be a bad time to show it to Officer Friendly and his pal Officer "Ponch" Poncherello.

STEP 4 ▸ GRAB ONE OF THEIR GUNS.

Do it. Come on! Live a little, you asshole. What's the worst that could happen? So they gun you down on your own doorstep. At least you won't have to clean up all those damn floaters after everyone leaves.

DON'T BE A DOUCHE

Don't actually grab the gun. I just feel I have to say that for legal reasons.

Get Better Seats at a Sporting Event

It's a beautiful day for baseball. Let's play two! Actually, I just peeked at your tickets. Watching two games that high up in the stadium might qualify you for frequent flyer miles.

The Problem

You want a closer view of the game, but buying new tickets is out of the question. The seats suck, but you're at least in the stadium for less scratch. You're going to have to sneak into the better sections without someone ratting you out and getting you escorted back to the bleachers by security.

The 'Hole Truth

It's going to take some greasing of the wheels and smooth talk, but if you play your cards right you could be sitting in the luxury boxes by the seventh-inning stretch. Here are some things to keep in mind when seat hopping in the stadium.

STEP 1 ▸ DON'T GO FOR BROKE THE FIRST TIME.

The big mistake people make is trying to sneak into the luxury boxes before the game even starts. Think about it, numbnuts; those seats are pretty damn expensive, so the chances of no one showing up to use them are pretty slim. Plus, you've already blown your cover in that section because now everyone around those seats knows you don't belong. Don't you feel stupid? If you don't, carrying around that foam finger should be all the reason you need.

STEP 2 ▸ TRY TO GREASE THE USHER.

It doesn't always work, because apparently some of these dudes take their job seriously, but you might be able to sneak into a better section for just a few extra bucks. Figure out which seats are empty and explain to the usher that those are your seats, but you just don't have your tickets (wink wink). Now hand over a twenty or fifty for his understanding.

STEP 3 ▸ DO SOME HOMEWORK USING YOUR PHONE.

Ah, the beauty of smart phones and the Internet: helping people cheat the system for almost a decade. Use your phone to pull up tickets for the day's game. Search for the best available seating. Write down the seat and section number and find it in the stadium. If there is no usher guarding, go right ahead and have a seat. No one is going to show up and tell you those are their seats, because no one bought the tickets.

STEP 4 ▸ ONCE YOU'RE IN, STAY IN.

If you get access and no one is bothering you, don't try your luck by getting up every five minutes or hassling the people around you, who actually paid for seats. Sit down, watch the game, and get up maybe once for a piss break and some food. On your way out, chat up the usher so he lets you come back without asking to see your stub.

Out-Asshole a Celebrity Asshole

It seems so much easier for the average Joe to rub elbows with celebrities today. It could be because regular people are now allowed into once exclusive places if they just make the right moves and pay enough money.

The Problem

You're out at bar when a celeb rolls in with a massive entourage. He is obviously getting a ton of attention from the other patrons and it's making you a little jealous. Remember, an asshole is always supposed to be the center of attention.

The 'Hole Truth

It's in your best interest to make contact with the celeb because it's all about who you know in this world. It's just not going to be easy, because everyone else in the place has the exact same idea in mind. Here is what you do.

STEP 1 ▸ DECIDE IF THE CELEB IS REALLY WORTH IT.

Is this person famous because of talent or because he or she was on a reality show, slept with someone famous, or slept with someone famous from a reality show? Anyone can get on a reality show (we'll explain how in the next entry), and this fame is probably fleeting. If you don't see the person staying famous in the next few years, don't even waste your time.

STEP 2 ▸ DON'T GO FOR THE BULL'S-EYE.

The mistake most people make when trying to cozy up to a celeb is aiming right for the celebrity. Never works. You've got to concentrate on peeling away the layers to eventually get to the center. Figure out who has access to the celeb but doesn't seem to be a part of the core group. Chat that person up and he or she will likely invite you over to meet the next ring on the target.

STEP 3 ▸ YOU HAVE NO IDEA WHO THE CELEBRITY IS.

Celebs often don't want to be celebs. They often just want to be treated just like everyone else. So treat them like everyone else. When you get introduced, act like you have no idea the person is even famous. Talk about anything but the celeb and even at one point forget his name. He won't remember yours anyway, so don't feel bad.

STEP 4 ▸ YOUR GOAL IS TO GET INVITED TO THE NEXT STOP.

This is the most important step. Since you're not a hot chick and you're not someone even more important than the celeb, he and the entourage are probably going to leave you at the bar while they jet-set off to another hot spot. You can't let this happen. You've got to get invited to the next place. This is how you know you're in. "It's cool, I'll follow the limo. I've got the red Honda Accord. I'll beep so you know it's me."

DON'T BE A DOUCHE

Don't be the guy who gets in a celeb's face just to start a fight. He is only trying to have a good time. Unless it's that dick tickler Spencer Pratt. Assholes get permission to knock him out.

Get on a Reality Show

Sadly, reality shows are the new fame-makers. Grab a copy of an entertainment rag and the cover is probably littered with people whose only claim to fame is the fact that a camera followed them around for three months while they mouth-humped numerous women or fist-pumped around a beach rental with a half dozen other goombahs.

The Problem
Only a douche bag has aspirations of willingly being on a reality show. It's incredibly shallow, but since you're not really talented at anything in particular (see the Build a Career with No Real Talent entry to find out why that

isn't a bad thing), your only shot at fifteen minutes of fame is getting on a reality show.

The 'Hole Truth

You can appear on a reality show and still come out with a shred of your pride. It all depends on the character you decide to portray and how you make your mark on the show.

STEP 1 ▸ TRY OUT FOR ALL THE SHOWS AS ONE OF THEIR STEREOTYPES.

Every show has the same character type but in different iterations: the good-looking player, the lunatic (or psycho chick), the frat boy (or party girl), the gay guy, the dork, and a couple other typical lifestyle choices that make it onto every show. You've just got to figure out which stereotypes they have already cast and fill in the void. Another option is to cram them all together and make yourself the good-looking player that drinks way too much and turns psycho because he has homoerotic fantasies about his dork friends. Smells like ratings gold.

STEP 2 ▸ STALK ONE CURRENTLY FILMING.

Every time a reality show goes into a town, there is a minor buzz from local news outlets. Find out where they are filming and where the cast hangs out at night and try to hook up with one of them. This would be a good time to test out that good-looking psycho role. It will get you on at least a few episodes.

STEP 3 ▸ PITCH YOUR OWN SHOW BUT CREATE THE CRAZY.

If you can't weasel your way into a reality show already on the air, try coming up with one of your own and pitch the idea around. You're either going to need a crazy job like ice fisherman or junk collector or have a serious screw loose, like hoarders or the druggies on *Intervention*. Now would be a good time to explore that shemale fetish. Do you wanna be on TV or not?

DON'T BE A DOUCHE

Honestly, it's easy to say don't be a douche, but people act completely different on camera. It's like a switch flicks on in their head and they do douchey stuff just to be interesting. I will forgive you for your douchey sins just for the couple months of filming. After that you have to be the good old asshole we know and love.

Get a Discount on Anything

Stores are dying for your business. Literally. Dying. Coughing and dying unless you start buying. Look at all the empty spots in the mall and on the street. They want your money so bad they are willing to take less of it just to make any profit. Advantage: asshole.

The Problem

You're making a big-ticket purchase that is going to considerably lighten your wallet. For this reason, you want to get the best price available and you've got no qualms about borderline begging for a deal.

The 'Hole Truth

Even if an item isn't technically on sale, there is always some room to haggle and get at least some money off.

OPTION 1 ▸ ALL YOU HAVE TO DO IS ASK.

Sometimes it's as simple as walking up to the register and saying "I don't want to pay full price. How can you help me?" Normally the salesperson will play ball and let you in on advertised deals you're unaware of or might have a coupon or two hanging around the register. If you're nice enough, she might hook you up with the "friends and family" discount that most employees get in major stores.

OPTION 2 ▸ FIND (OR MAKE) A FLAW.

You're going to purchase a new sport coat or a button-down shirt for a date but ohhh, look at that—it's missing a button on the bottom. Damn, and it's the only one in your size. Maybe the store will give you a discount on the damaged material. Oh, and hang on to the button. You're going to have to sew that on when you get home.

OPTION 3 ▸ GATHER INSIDE INTELLIGENCE.

Salespeople know when sales are coming. It's part of their job. They also try not to work at that time because the place is a madhouse. Ask an employee if he knows when the item is expected to go on sale. Some of them might toe the company line and say they "can't divulge that information," so just go ask another employee until you get an answer.

OPTION 4 ▸ EVEN THOUGH YOU BOUGHT IT, KEEP SHOPPING.

Let's say you make the purchase and you get a decent deal. Keep an eye on circulars and online sales. If the item goes on sale anywhere from thirty to ninety days after you bought it, most stores will honor the sale price and give you the rest of the money back. If they don't, return it with the original receipt, get all your money back, and buy it cheaper.

OPTION 5 ▸ MAKE A SCENE.

Salespeople hate it when you cause a ruckus around other customers. This is exactly why you should cause a ruckus around other customers if you don't get what you've asked for. Explain how loyal of a customer you've been over the years and how much money you spend, talking incredibly loud so the entire store can hear you. The salesperson will probably give you any discount just to get you out of the store. If she calls the manager, get even louder and the manager will do something to "make it all up to you." The customer is always right, especially if he is an asshole.

DON'T BE A DOUCHE

Don't take it out on the help. If they can't give you a discount it's likely not their fault. Just ask to see someone who does have the power.

Create Your Own Wikipedia Page

You aren't important if you don't have a Wikipedia page. It's where 99 percent of people go on the Internet to gather what they feel is actual, factual information. Most of it is bullshit and completely fabricated, but it's only important that people think it's true.

The Problem
You don't have a Wikipedia page. You can't convince anyone to make one about you and you certainly don't think anyone is going to do it based on the fact that they think you are worthy of an entry.

The 'Hole Truth
A Wikipedia page is vital to your dating life, future job opportunities, and any other reason people would have to search your name on the Internet. "Oh, wow, this guy has his own Wikipedia page. He must be a real somebody." Here is how to score your own slice of the Internet.

STEP 1 ▸ ALL YOU NEED IS ONE GOOD REASON.
The lead paragraph should really convince people that you deserve your own page. If you've accomplished something amazing in life you're all set, but if you haven't, it's time to fabricate just a smidge. Pick an accomplishment that isn't easily researched, or one that

people wouldn't spend time looking up anyway. Make yourself part of a larger group so that your membership would be hard to dispute. "First to march with Martin Luther King. Worked on Reagan's re-election staff. Original staff writer for the show *Arli$$*."

STEP 2 ▸ TRY TO BE OBJECTIVE.

Your page must be objective. You can't go on and on bragging about the wonderful man that is you because people will sniff it out in a second. Act like you're writing an obituary. Be boring in tone and content.

STEP 3 ▸ MAKE SURE TO CITE REFERENCES.

You can't just link to one place, like your own website or a Tumblr account you started about the funny shit a squirrel thinks about while running around the yard. You've got to cite other sources to make the information look credible. If you're claiming to be an original member of The Commodores, link out to their Wikipedia page. That was easy. Easy like Sunday morning.

STEP 4 ▸ MAKE AT LEAST ONE OUTLANDISH CLAIM.

It's acceptable. Everyone knows that almost every Wikipedia page has at least one ridiculous claim. Shoot for the moon. Actually, that's a good one. "Once shot the moon on a bet by Jesus." People can't say it didn't happen.

⊢ **DON'T BE A DOUCHE** ⊢

Jesus would never make such a silly wager.

To keep the Wikipedia page alive, have other people add information. Of course, this can lead to people putting less-than-flattering things about you on the page, but that's the risk you take when you have your own section in the only source of information people rely on anymore.

Borrow Money without Ever Paying It Back

Even assholes run a little low on cash. Living the life gets expensive. An asshole does share the wealth, but sometimes that wealth isn't as large as the asshole makes it appear. Cash flow runs low.

The Problem

It's a couple days from payday and the bank account is a couple dimes under an Abe Lincoln. You've got a few things planned that are going to take some serious cash, and don't want to put it all on a charge.

The 'Hole Truth

You can still have a good time on somebody's dime and work your way into never paying it back. You'll need to offer something in return, because only a douche bag would take a person's money and never even things out. That's just bad karma.

STEP 1 ▸ FRIENDS FIRST, THEN FAMILY, THEN STRANGERS.

It's common practice to hit up family for money. It's never the best idea. If you keep hitting them up for cash, and never paying it back, it causes a rift that could end with a family divided. This is bad because family is important to an asshole. It keeps him grounded. Lending money is something friends do.

STEP 2 ▸ KEEP THE DENOMINATION DIGESTIBLE.

There is nothing worse than a douche bag who asks for way more money than he needs "just in case." Crunch the numbers and even go so far as to present them to the lender. If you only need a couple hundred bucks, that's all you should request. A smaller amount makes it easier to swallow when forking it over and when your friend never sees it back in his account.

STEP 3 ▸ BARTER.

Thou shalt not covet thy neighbor's new Beamer or half-rental by the beach. But we do. There is a possession of yours that your pal has had his eye on for a long time. You've got to offer it up as collateral. If you don't have worldly possessions, offer services in exchange for cash. Whoa! Not those types of services. Offer to help him move, get him access to events or contacts, and even offer your body up for uncomfortable grunt work. Ugh. Painting or lawn care, you deviant. Honestly, is everything sexual with you, Paulie Pervy?

STEP 4 ▸ BE HONEST.

Tell your friend there is a good chance he may never see this money again. It's then up to him to take the chance of giving you the scratch. It's a form of gambling. He'll put down the money but knows there is a 50/50 chance it's gone for good. Actually, 50/50 is probably some of the best odds a person can get when betting money. Those odds would make slot machines much more enjoyable.

⊢ DON'T BE A DOUCHE ⊢

You should only borrow money from a friend once without paying it back. Trick him once, shame on him. Trick him twice, you should lose a pint of blood in the melee.

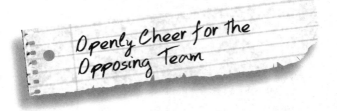

Openly Cheer for the Opposing Team

An asshole loves his team. Loyal to a fault. The problem is he can't always live near the home stadium or travel back, so he is forced to catch the squad at his local venue. In other words, he must invade enemy territory.

The Problem

There are some stadiums where you can waltz right up to the ticket booth on game day and score seats behind the dugout to harass the home team or even block off a section for an entire busload of out-of-towners, but pulling that off in cities like New York, Philly, and Oakland might have you bleeding a lot more than just your team colors.

The 'Hole Truth

Cheering for the opposing team is a dangerous proposition, but if you handle it correctly you could survive to see the end of the game.

STEP 1 ▸ TRAVEL WITH A GROUP (POSSIBLY WITH A FEW HOME FANS MIXED IN).

Remember that there is safety in numbers. The bigger the group, the less likelihood of anyone starting static. This allows you to be pretty vocal about how much you love your team and how much penis the other team enjoys to suck. The safety in numbers only works when entering and exiting the stadium—unless all twenty of you can figure out how to get a beer at the same time or simultaneously piss in the same urinal. If you're a big enough asshole, the opposing mongrels will wait until you're alone.

STEP 2 ▸ MAKE FRIENDS WITH THE PEOPLE IN YOUR SEATING AREA.

Don't be a douche before the game even starts. You could regret it if your team starts taking an ass-beating on the field and you've been mouthing off since warm-ups. During the down time, make friends with the hometown fans in your section. Playfully tell them you're going to bust their balls all night and that there shouldn't be any hard feelings. They should feel free to do the same thing in the event that your team shits the bed. Making nice with the surrounding fans could come in handy later in the evening should you find yourself in trouble with other fans who've wandered over to your section to shove an entire box of Fiddle Faddle down your gullet.

STEP 3 ▸ KNOW WHEN TO PIPE DOWN.

You'll realize when the situation is getting out of control. You should be the wiser asshole in the situation, knowing when to dial things back a little bit for the sake of safety. You might be in control, but everyone knows the plethora drunk douche bags hang out at ballparks with nothing better to do but start fights and knock out teeth. They want to get something out of this expensive ticket; they are losing a day's pay at Walgreens to go to the game.

STEP 4 ▸ IT'S NOT WORTH GOING TO JAIL OVER.

Remember, the whole argument started over a game played by grown men getting paid millions of dollars to do so. They don't give a turd about you or the fact that you're showing your pride in the team colors by getting repeatedly kicked in the throat by a gang of other fans. For you it's all just for fun. Nothing to go to jail or lose a limb over. Unless of course it's the championship game and your team is getting their ass handed to them. Then it's just a release of the anguish of being so close to a trophy and then losing.

DON'T BE A DOUCHE

It's one thing to gloat when the team is winning, but to be an insufferable douche if your team loses . . . well, that just looks like you're trying to pick a fight. But maybe you are, so in that case, start swinging because SOMEONE wearing the jersey should come out a winner today. Start clubbing women and children first, or use them as a human shield. Okay, just kidding. Mostly.

Have the Most Fun at a Bachelor Party

A bachelor party is meant to honor (and say goodbye) to the bachelor lifestyle of the guy getting hitched. While the groom is guaranteed to at least have a decent time (mainly because he doesn't have to spend a dime all night), the rest of the party might not have the *Hangover* experience because the locale and activities are border-line high-school antics—drinking at a guy's house, playing video games, and hitting up a bar you've been to a hundred times. Color yourself bored shitless.

The Problem

You're in the middle of a bachelor party that is about as fun as a funeral mass. Minus the wine and free bread crisps. You've got to liven the party up fast or find another group to party with for the rest of the night.

The 'Hole Truth

It doesn't matter if the bachelor is having a hoot. You should only be concerned with your own amusement right now. Especially for the amount of cash you dropped down for this snoozer. Get your noisemakers and cone-shaped hats, it's time to head up the party planning committee.

STEP 1 ▸ USE THE GROOM.

He is an instant conversation starter wherever you go. A gaggle of hot chicks walks by your party? Seize the moment. "Hey girls, this guy is getting married, got any advice?" They will stick around for at least a couple minutes. Tell the bouncer, the waitress, the bartender, and anyone who looks like they can hand you some freebies that you're a bachelor party and plan on spending a ton of cash. They might comp you some stuff for this visit or possibly a future visit.

STEP 2 ▸ BREAK OFF INTO A SMALLER GROUP.

A big problem with bachelor parties is that often they're much too big of a group. Running with a pack of fifteen or twenty guys is hard to handle because every guy has a different opinion on what to do and where to go next. Too many cooks spoil the pot. Actually, too many smoke the pot, but that is an issue for another time. Figure out the guys in the group who will have the most fun and quietly break away from the clan when no one is paying attention.

STEP 3 ▸ PRETEND TO BE THE GROOM.

If he isn't reaping all the rewards for the group, step in and do it for him. Approach the manager of the place and tell him you're upset with—ehh, pick anything— and ask how he plans on remedying the situation. If the groom splits off from the party into another group or calls it an early night, take over the role of catalyst and keep the party going as the "groom" for the rest of the guys. It's sad when a bachelor party is still hanging without an actual groom in sight.

STEP 4 ▸ GET SHITFACED!

Honestly, is there any situation Johnnie Walker or Jim Beam can't solve? They need their own *CSI* spinoff, they are that good. When you're drunk, anything seems fun, even when it really is awful. Drink enough and you'll erase the night from your mind. Another option is to get everyone else off-their-balls hammered and observe while they stumble around and puke on their polos.

DON'T BE A DOUCHE

Make it as easy as possible on the groom until the bachelor party gets under way. Answer the e-mails, go along with the plans, and pay up accordingly if money is collected prior to the activity. Don't be a douche and make it hard on the groom or the guy planning the event. There will be time to bust his balls when you find out the bachelor party sucks.

Take a Vacation

Every asshole needs time to unwind. Disconnect from the real world and just veg out in a tropical climate for at least a week. Get the batteries recharged and prepare for another couple months of battling life day after day. The sad fact is people just don't know how to take an actual vacation anymore.

The Problem

People know how to go away; they just don't know how to get away. When you're on vacation, the real world shouldn't exist. It should be a million miles away in distance and in thought. Unfortunately, your douche of a boss, annoying friends, and mother who thinks your cell phone is a free pass to call you at all hours of the day (and night) don't understand the idea you're not "available" for the next few days.

The 'Hole Truth

You've got to take control and cut yourself off from the civilized world. Think *Lost* or *Gilligan's Island* without the hot movie star and slutty farmer chick. No phones, no lights, no motorcars, and whatever else that damn theme song said. Here's how to escape.

STEP 1 ▸ DON'T TELL ANYONE WHERE THE HELL YOU'RE GOING.

Does the boss, your neighbor, or anyone else have to know which island you're flying to or the hotel you're staying in? What can they possibly do with that information besides bother you for reasons they feel are important but are really just bullshit that can be handled when you get home? Tell only one extremely trustworthy person where you're going, and tell everyone else in case of emergency to contact that person, who can decide whether you really need to be reached.

STEP 2 ▸ ALL YOU NEED ARE CLOTHES AND MONEY.

The laptop can stay home, the cell phone in the room and only for emergencies, and your eReader can stay on your coffee table because apparently books are now available in paper form. Who would have thought? Leave all connections to the outside world far from your piña colada–scented fingers.

STEP 3 ▸ GO ALONE.

If you're married with kids, fine, I guess take them, but for every other situation you should take off for paradise solo. No need to take a date along when there are plenty of available women where you're going. And don't go with friends, because you'll want to choke them out by the second day. Just be alone for a while.

⊢ DON'T BE A DOUCHE ⊢

Pick a grown-up destination for your excursion. If you're too old for spring break and way too old for Disney, choose a place where other adults hang out.

Chapter 7.

Asshole Essentials

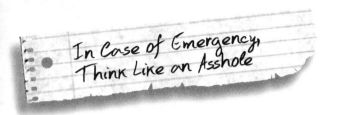

In Case of Emergency,
Think Like an Asshole

An asshole has to be prepared for anything; natural disaster, act of terrorism, running out of coffee after a hangover, or any major hurdle that this world might toss at his feet. Only the strong survive because the strong are usually the assholes in the group.

The Problem

You're faced with a major crisis situation and there could be some casualties. It's no fun being dead. You don't want to try it, not even for a second. Everyone is panicking and it's only making matters worse. You're going to have to take matters into your own hands.

The 'Hole Truth

You can beat this if you think smart. You've got to keep calm while using all you've learned in your asshole training (along with some basic common survival skills) to maneuver the situation and come out alive on the other side. You will make it out alive if you follow four steps.

> **STEP 1 ▶ REMEMBER DEMANDMENT I:**
> **YOU ONLY CARE ABOUT YOURSELF.**
>
> In the end, the only person who matters is you, so do everything in your power to survive the situation. If you've got to do something that looks dangerous, let someone else attempt it first. If you can save another life by sacrificing your own, don't do it; let someone else be the hero.

STEP 2 ▶ DO THE OPPOSITE OF THE CROWD.

Ever notice that in moments of panic and stress, people do the dumbest things and end up getting themselves killed? Or worse, they do something stupid and convince many other people to do the same thing only to see a large group end up dead. Don't be a sheep. If something seems like an awful idea, it usually is, no matter how many people are willing to try it. Let them all perish. It will leave room for the smart people who want to live.

STEP 3 ▶ FEED OFF THE ADRENALINE.

Adrenaline is a power narcotic that will turn the average man into a raging beast at the right moment. Use the influx of adrenaline to keep yourself sharp and alive. Keep telling yourself "I'm gonna make it through this," and let the adrenaline guide you to safety. If something, or someone, is standing in your way, just run through it or over it to get to safety.

STEP 4 ▶ STUPID WILL GET YOU KILLED.

Before every decision, ask yourself, "Is this a really dumb idea?" It's okay to have a dumb idea in the moments of sheer panic. It's just not good to act on those dumb ideas. Use the headline rule: If you die doing this, will the headline make you look stupid? "Area man jumps from window using tablecloth as handheld parachute, plunges to death." That reads like a really dumb idea, doesn't it?

╎ DON'T BE A DOUCHE ╎

Don't encourage others to do things that may get them killed. If you don't agree with their idea, just go your own way. No one needs a douche pushing them toward an early grave.

Face Off! How To Handle Another Asshole

You weren't the only person who read the first book (thank Christ, because I would have had to pay back the advance). There is a good chance you're going to run into a fellow asshole in the field of battle. Some will be accommodating and greet you with a handshake and a nod of approval, but others will consider you a threat and look to knock you down.

The Problem

You're out having a good time when you get a strange feeling. A chill up your spine. A cold wind. A hushed crowd. There is another asshole in the room. You suddenly make eye contact as you spot him rubbing the goose bumps on his neck. Asshole meets asshole. That sounds like homosexual porno. Two assholes collide. Okay, this is just getting worse. You see what I'm getting at.

The 'Hole Truth

It's like a shootout in the Old West. Two assholes standing just steps apart, each ready to blow the other off the face of the Earth if the other guy makes one move for his pistol. Man, I could not make this all sound more gay if I tried. Ugh. Here is what to do depending on whether the asshole turns out to be a friend or foe.

IF HE IS A FRIEND . . .

It's the perfect time to join forces and harness the power that only two assholes together can possess. First discuss how much you loved the first book. Go ahead, I will wait. Shit, that didn't take long. Anyway, it's always good to have another asshole in your corner in any social situation. Together you can dominate the room and feast on the bounty that is a stuffed bean burrito with a side of rice and beans and . . . oh, sorry, I was ordering lunch. Did you want something?

IF HE IS AN ENEMY . . .

Cut him down before he has a chance to do the same to you. Start to influence and infiltrate everyone in his circle. Get them into your favor one by one. Make him feel alone and vulnerable. You have him exactly where you want him. You now have the upper hand. You can either approach him and claim victory or let him suffer a little more while you bask in your aura of assholeness. It's fun to make him suffer, so let it drag out for as long as possible.

IF YOU JUST DON'T CARE EITHER WAY . . .

The world is big enough for several assholes. You don't have to like everyone, and not everyone has to like you. Yes, this is the same pep talk you got after you got beat up at summer camp.

IF YOU'VE BEEN FOOLED AND HE IS ACTUALLY A GIANT DOUCHE . . .

Punch him in the throat.

Appendix—*Cheat Sheet* Tips and Quips

TAKE-HOME ASSIGNMENT:

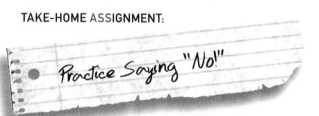

Practice Saying "No!"

An asshole must learn to say the word "no" in many situations. It's not always easy. To practice, for the next week, say no to these five people. It doesn't matter the situation. Pretend it's crack, and Nancy Reagan is standing over your shoulder. Just say no!

Your Mother—It's hard to say no to mom, but think of all the times she said no to you when you were growing up. Remember that co-ed sleepover you missed in the ninth grade? Yeah, you're still bitter. You missed some teen titties.

Children—Those precious little faces. Especially when they pout or get sad. It will melt your cold heart. If you're a pussy. Say no. It's good for them. It builds character.

The Homeless—Half of them are scammers, and the other half are just lazy. Saying no is actually better than the custom of ignoring them on the street. That's just a douche-bag move. Say no but wish them luck. It's a more asshole thing to do. Unless they are yelling crazy shit; then just ignore them.

Pets—They won't understand the actual word "no" (especially when you do that NO! NOOOOOOOO bull-crap) but they will get it when you don't pet them, give them treats, or let them in the house.

Yourself—This is the greatest test of all. It's hard to tell yourself no when you really want something. Look at your reflection in the mirror and say no. It's hard. You've got a honest little face. Fine. Just this once say yes, but I'm not sure a man your age belongs at a ninth-grade sleepover.

TAKE-HOME ASSIGNMENT:

Perfect the Backhanded Compliment

You've done incredibly well for yourself thus far, considering your lack of talent and charisma. See what I did there? Said something nice, only to WHAM! put you down in the same breath. The backhanded compliment is an important tool in the asshole utility belt. Learn how to think on your feet to deliver the perfect backhanded compliment in any situation. Here are some good examples.

"Wow, you look fantastic for such a big fan of fudge."

"Your mother must be so proud."

"I've never met a person so happy to be average."

"Your baby is much cuter than I would have expected."

"That is a great dress! It really takes attention away from your problem areas."

"Sex was amazing once I showed you how."

"Your answers are always perfectly adequate."

"You're incredibly attractive. It's great, because your voice had me nervous."

"This is a fantastic book from men of such little talent."

TAKE-HOME ASSIGNMENT:

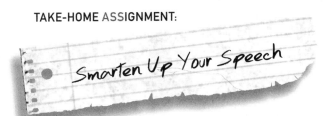

Smarten Up Your Speech

An asshole is always learning new phrases and dropping them into daily conversation. It's important to use them correctly, or you just look dumber and would be better off not knowing the word at all. Here are some new words to add to your personal vernacular, including their definition and the right and wrong way to use them in a sentence. Also, go look up "vernacular." You look puzzled.

Consternation, noun: amazement or dismay that hinders or throws into confusion

CORRECT: *"The two men stared at each other in consternation, neither knowing how to react."*

INCORRECT: *"Those cookies you brought to work had me consternated for three days. I need some fiber."*

Incontrovertible, adj.: not open to question

CORRECT: *"The new vacation rules handed down by Human Resources are incontrovertible, so save your breath."*

INCORRECT: *"On sunny days I like to drive my incontrovertible into the office with the top down."*

Juxtaposition, noun: the act or an instance of placing two or more things side by side; also, the state of being so placed

CORRECT: *"It is the result of the juxtaposition of contrasting colors."*

INCORRECT: *"I want to sleep with the new intern in her car, juxtapositioning her long legs over my shoulders."*

Punitive, adj.: inflicting, involving, or aiming at punishment

CORRECT: *"That demotion is going to have a punitive effect on his ability to work."*

INCORRECT: *"These tight pants make my package look punitive."*

Ramification, noun: the consequences or outgrowth of a decision

CORRECT: *"Show up late to work one more time and there will be ramifications."*

INCORRECT: *"Sally from the company next door just got a new pair of boobs. She has definitely shot up the ramification scale."*

NECESSARY ASS-CESSORY:

The Business Card

The business card is an asshole's ticket into, and out of, every situation.

Into: Business card hand-offs mean new clients, golf pals, and possibly bed buddies of the female persuasion.

Out of: It's the stock non sequitur that effectively ends any dull conversation. "Did I tell you about my trip to Belize?" "No, but did I tell you that I gotta leave? Shoot me the pics via e-mail." Hand him the card. Convo ended. Then go home and delete that e-mail and its attachments. He looks horrendous in a two-piece.

Every asshole knows: You should have a business card and a personal card. Business for networking and personal for weddings, funerals, and "accidentally" disrupting a Women and Sex Addiction self-help group at the community center.

Keep it brief: Name. Number. E-mail. Stifle the social media account info.

DON'T BE A DOUCHE

Learn when to give someone the business (card). Stop selling yourself. It's offensive, much like your natural scent.

NECESSARY ASS-CESSORY:

Picture with Someone Famous

Every asshole needs a photo standing next to a famous person. The more famous the person, the more important you become in the eyes of . . . hell, everyone. It should be prominently displayed in your home, office, or on the dashboard of your car.

Here are five famous people to get snapped with to cement your status as an asshole to be revered.

Bill Clinton—Women love Slick Willie, and he might just be the most powerful asshole to ever hold the office. Guys love him too. It's also impressive that you got so close to a man who once ruled the free world. He looks like he smells of women's perfume. Can you confirm?

Carrot Top—The man is a loose cannon. He is also a conversation starter. Everyone will want to know the story of how you met Carrot Top.

The Dalai Lama—Double bonus points if you can get him to do something funny, like the rock 'n' roll devil horns or the shocker hand gesture.

The most interesting man in the world—The guy from the Dos Equis ad. That makes you cool enough to pose with the most interesting man in the world. You don't always drink beer, but when you do, it's with this guy.

The gerbil that made Richard Gere infamous—Find him. Take a picture with him. He may still be deep up the orifice and only comes out once a year, like the groundhog from Pennsylvania. You wait his ass out.

DOUBLE BONUS—Take a picture with this book's author. Please? It would mean a lot to me and my publisher.

RETROSPECTIVE:

The Decade's Biggest Assholes

James Frey—Bestselling author and literary punching bag, Frey made headlines after the Smoking Gun exposed "A Million Little Lies" about the inaccuracies of the author's book, *A Million Little Pieces.* The site alleged that Frey fabricated large parts of his memoir, including details about his criminal record and a train accident that never happened. He even pissed off Oprah, which is something to which every asshole should aspire.

Gordon Ramsay—A world-renowned chef, Ramsay has been awarded a total of sixteen Michelin Stars. I only know that because I looked it up on Wikipedia. Guess that makes him a big deal. The guy gets paid to be an asshole on TV in two different countries.

Bill Belichick—The biggest sourpuss to ever walk a sideline, Belichick carries on the tradition of the asshole coach who isn't there to make friends with players or pal around with reporters. He has better things to do, like win five Super Bowls (two as New York Giants defensive coordinator and three as New England Patriots head coach).

Harvey Levin/TMZ—Do I really want to know that celeb A left celeb B's house at 2 A.M., or watch minor celebrity X stumble out of a nightclub and start throwing punches at people? TMZ knows that I do. The TMZ cameras catch celebs being assholes, all while acting like assholes themselves.

Kobe Bryant—Bryant became almost an instant star but not exactly a team player. In 2003 Bryant was accused of sexual assault, and admitted to an adulterous sexual encounter with the accuser, but denied sexually assaulting her. He smoothed it all over with a "Kobe Ring" to his wife. "Sorry I nailed that chick. Here's a ring the size of Jupiter."

Bacon—Can a food product be an asshole? Yes. Let's see . . . a bacon bra, bacon martinis, and bacon ice cream, just to name a few. If you name it, it's probably been baconed. Know what else is great about bacon? It knows it's bad for you and doesn't really give a shit.

Brett Favre—The Brett Favre saga played out every spring and summer for most of the decade and saturated the sports media. Partly due to ESPN and sports radio talking heads, Favre spent more time in the headlines during the off-season than he did during the four months of the actual football season. None of it was really his fault. It's easy for celebs and athletes to blame the media, but in Favre's case he was just trying to decide whether to play football or not.

Tiger Woods—If I had put together this list two weeks before that magical Thanksgiving night, Tiger might have been included solely for his attitude and accolades on the golf course. Then along came mistresses #1 through #36. Holy turds, how did this guy find the time? I'm thinking the injury that kept him off the course most of 2009 was a pulled penis, not a bum knee.

FAQs

Really? Two of these books? Was that necessary?

It was not only necessary; it was demanded by the legions of assholes around the world. Every asshole should have been ready for #2 to drop. See what I did there?

Can a woman be an asshole?

Yes, a woman can indeed be an asshole. In some cases she is instead referred to as a bitch, but there is a huge difference between the two behaviors. A bitch has many of the traits of an asshole, but is generally not well liked by either gender, whereas an asshole is still well liked despite his (or her) actions. A woman is better off acting like an asshole, because it's more accepted by both men and women. A bitch is much closer to a douche bag. This is making me consider some type of chart or diagram for visual purposes. Maybe next book.

Being an asshole got me (insert a type of bodily harm). Was that supposed to happen?

It wasn't supposed to happen, but I'm shocked it doesn't happen to assholes more often. It just means you were doing something right—you pissed someone off enough to inflict bodily harm. I should probably start including sections about good health care providers.

How soon is too soon to ask a widow on a date?

It all depends on how her husband died. If you ask her out too soon after he was in a car accident or fire, then you're being a douche bag. If he kicked the bucket because of a heart attack, stroke, or any other medical ailment, you can ask her out in the cafeteria of the hospital. If she says no, try some of the ladies hanging around the ICU.

Is it an asshole or a douche-bag move to tip less than 5 percent if you'll never be back to the restaurant?

It's a tough call. I'd first say asshole because you're saving your money, which an asshole should always do, but it's a douche-bag move because a waiter lives off tips and he served your ass for the last hour for a measly couple bucks. I can't decide, so I'm just going to call you an ass bag and split the difference. Just hope he didn't spooze in your food, because "you'll never be back again."

What are some other books an asshole should read/own besides *Assholeology: The Science Behind Getting Your Way and Getting Away With It* and *Assholeology: The Cheat Sheet?*

Excellent question. I recommend furthering your asshole knowledge by reading *The 48 Laws of Power*, by Robert Greene; *The Maxims of Manhood,* by Jeff Wilser; and *Touch Me: The Poems of Suzanne Somers*.

Is there an official asshole mascot?

You mean like one of those cartoony characters you see running around baseball stadiums? Should there be? I hadn't really thought about it. Does anyone want to see a cartoon version of an asshole? Wouldn't it look like two walnuts with traces of brownie on their shell? Ugh, I just grossed myself out. You need to retract that question.

This book was in the humor section of the bookstore. Shouldn't it be in self-help?

It should be in every section of the bookstore because it's just that goddamn important. It can be considered a business book, a self-help book, a biography of sorts, a romance novel, and even a children's book. Every book is a children's book if the child can read.

Is it true that if you ask a girl if she's taken it in the dumper and the response is anything other than "NO," then she has?

Holy letter to *Penthouse!* What the hell kind of question is that? Take that stuff to Dr. Drew on *Loveline.* That isn't a topic I'm at liberty to discuss. When you find out, let me know, because now I'm curious.

How come neither book is a movie yet?

Totally! I was thinking the same thing. It just needs a solid script. Bradley Cooper could play the quintessential asshole. His love interest could be every hot chick in Hollywood under the age of twenty-five. The only request is that the authors get a small cameo in the movie. Maybe a speaking line or two. Couple million dollars should cover everything.

Does an asshole ever do karaoke?

Not unless he knows an Asian stripper named Karaoke.

Is it true Tucker Max blocked you on Twitter?

Yup. What a douche bag.

About the Author

Chris Illuminati is a lucky bastard. After toiling around for years in jobs he hated, he just decided one day to be a writer. He tricked people into thinking he was talented. He is one clever asshole.

Illuminati has been a regular online contributor to sites like Ask Men, The Bachelor Guy, EgoTV, and Asylum and to magazines like *Penthouse* and *Details*. He writes about dating, sex, marriage, pop culture, and how clueless he is when it comes to raising a child. He lives in New Jersey with his wife, son, and a cat named Stephen.

DAILY BENDER

Want Some More?

Hit up our humor blog, The Daily Bender, to get your fill of all things funny—be it subversive, odd, offbeat, or just plain mean. The Bender editors are there to get you through the day and on your way to happy hour. Whether we're linking to the latest video that made us laugh or calling out (or bullshit on) whatever's happening, we've got what you need for a good laugh.

If you like our book, you'll love our blog. (And if you hated it, "man up" and tell us why.) Visit The Daily Bender for a shot of humor that'll serve you until the bartender can.

Sign up for our newsletter at
www.adamsmedia.com/blog/humor
and download our Top Ten Maxims No Man Should Live Without.